AF516648

Taste

7 Michelin Star and Celebrity Chefs

Compiled & Edited by

Anand Kapoor

Om Books International

Published in 2013 by

Om Books International

Corporate & Editorial Office
A-12, Sector 64, Noida 201 301
Uttar Pradesh, India
Phone: +91 120 477 4100
Email: editorial@ombooks.com
Website: www.ombooksinternational.com

Sales Office
4379/4B, Prakash House, Ansari Road
Darya Ganj, New Delhi 110 002, India
Phone: +91 11 2326 3363, 2326 5303
Fax: +91 11 2327 8091
Email: sales@ombooks.com
Website: www.ombooks.com

Text © Respective Contributors

Editors
Shreya Chakravertty & Ipshita Sengupta Nag
Design & Layout
Shraboni Roy & Ratnakar Singh
Photographers
Anjum Anand: Lisa Barber; Frances Atkins: Sue Hiscoe; Ian Curley: Jana Liebenstein;
Laurie Gear: Lisa Barber; Marcello Tully: Andrew and Rosie Woodhouse;
Vikas Khanna: Diana DeLucia; Vineet Bhatia: Lisa Barber; Anand Kapoor: Sue Hiscoe

© Om Books International 2013

All rights reserved. No part of this book may be reproduced or transmitted in any form by any means, electronic or mechanical, including photocopying and recording, or by any information storage and retrieval system, except as may be expressly permitted in writing by the publisher.

ISBN: 978-93-83202-05-8

Printed in India by Ajanta Offset & Packagings Ltd., New Delhi

10 9 8 7 6 5 4 3 2 1

For every child who has a dream

Contents

Introduction

Cooking is a labour of love. The desire to create something and present it to another person is an act of pure nurturing and honesty, leaving you open to rejection or appreciation. Food is evocative; it has an emotive charge: you may be stuck in traffic or another stressful situation but a certain taste or aroma can turn you into a 10-year-old child and transport you back in time to your mother's kitchen.

My journey in the culinary world began from a young age—when I realised food and the processes involved in its preparation could be used to bring people together and impart a sense of community. While at school, I became determined to learn the trade. I worked in various restaurants, ranging from fast food outlets to fine dining establishments. But as I worked, I realised being a professional chef was a lot harder than I had ever imagined. I resigned myself to my destiny—that of being an amateur home cook.

During this time, I discovered that food doesn't have to be complicated to be enjoyable—simple recipes using store-bought ingredients can be just as delicious as the most lavish dining experiences. My brief stint in the food industry also gave me a raft of recipes that I have carried with me through life. I have included the ones closest to my heart in *Taste: 7 Michelin Star and Celebrity Chefs.*

'Give a man a fish and he eats for a day; teach a man to fish and he can feed himself for life'—this Chinese proverb underlines the basic aim we all have every time we enter a kitchen—self-sustenance. In the most essential terms, we all need food to survive. Therefore, the royalties from the sale of *Taste* shall be used to support the Creative Services Support Group (CSSG), a registered charity and organisation that aims at the progressive development of the underprivileged through skill-training and mentorship in various creative sectors in order to enable them to earn a sustainable livelihood.

The book came about through a series of fortunate coincidences. I had been wanting to create a cookbook that was beautiful enough to be displayed on a coffee table and set out as a series of menus by Michelin Star chefs. On a chance meeting, publisher Ajay Mago of Om Books International fell equally in love with the idea and swiftly moved it forward. It is with his vision, and the hard work of my co-editors Shreya Chakravertty and Ipshita Sengupta Nag that the book has come together. Shraboni Roy and Ratnakar Singh worked quietly to create an elegant design.

We have been lucky to bring some of the best chefs in the world on board for *Taste.*

Anjum Anand's intelligence and clarity of mind is reflected in the way she cooks. A genuine star and very down to earth, Anjum has been one of the foremost supporters of the charity from the days of its establishment. She has brought a wealth of global knowledge to her cooking and has distilled it into easy-to-follow, nutritious and delicious dishes.

In my desperate bid to find another woman chef to be part of the book, I realised that they are still outnumbered by men in the professional culinary world. **Frances Atkins** came to my rescue. And it is amazing to see her in action in the kitchen—she is in total control yet has a gentle hand that is directly reflected in her food. A trip to The Yorke Arms in Yorkshire is definitely worth its while.

I contacted **Ian Curley** via email for *Taste* and he genuinely thought it was a joke—a manifestation of his straightforward and unfussy self. His style of cooking has these admirable qualities too. He has created an empire at The European in Melbourne and remains true to his roots while conjuring up his food magic.

Vineet Bhatia has commendable attributes to his credit, apart from his cooking wizardry. A loving and doting family man, he is always ready for fresh challenges. The powerhouse behind him and his restaurant in London, Rasoi, is his wife Rashima, the pillar that he leans on.

Another two gentlemen who greatly derive their strength from their wives, Jacqueline and Claire, respectively, are **Laurie Gear** and **Marcello Tully.** Both are from different ends of the UK—Laurie's restaurant, The Artichoke, is in the south of England while Marcello's retreat, Kinloch Lodge, is on the island of Skye—and the genuineness in their cooking touches the hearts of one and all. They source most of their ingredients locally and put up plates that are beautiful to look at as well as a treat for the taste buds.

Vikas Khanna was an enthusiastic recruit for *Taste* and he pulled out all the stops to assist us in our venture. Passionate about his roots in Amritsar, his restaurant, Junoon, in New York is a must visit.

The supporting cast in any kind of venture is always invaluable. Mine has been my wife, my parents, my brother and my kids. Without all of them in the background, this book would not have been possible.

For all the chefs and talented photographers who have contributed to this book, thank you for your support.

Enjoy cooking.

Anand Kapoor, 2013

Anjum Anand

Celebrity chef Anjum Anand is a popular face of UK television and has enthralled her audience for a decade now with her healthy recipes and engaging personality. She grew up in London and has worked in various innovative kitchens around the world. Anjum can be given credit for being one of the pioneers of simplifying traditional rich Indian cooking into simple, wholesome meals. Determined to promote the concept of a healthy body, Anjum has authored several books on eating right. In 2007, Anjum made her first television appearance with the series Indian Food Made Easy on BBC 2. In 2008 a second series was commissioned and was watched by over 3 million viewers. Both series have established Anjum's expertise as a top class chef.

Recipes

Coconut French Toast

Serves 2

Ingredients

4 slices of brioche or the sliced bread
2 eggs
200 ml plain milk
6 tbsp desiccated coconut
3 tbsp sugar (use only 2 tbsp if you are going to serve with jaggery coconut syrup or any other syrup)
2 tbsp vegetable oil
2 knobs butter
oil and butter to cook

- Whisk together the eggs, milk and sugar. Spread the desiccated coconut on a small plate.
- Heat the oil and butter in a large non-stick frying pan over a medium flame. Dip one slice in the batter for about 30-40 seconds, pressing lightly to help the bread absorb the batter. Place on the desiccated coconut and press gently, then turn and coat the next side.
- Place straight in the hot pan and repeat with the other slice. Cook on a moderate flame until golden; around 2 minutes. Carefully flip over and brown the other side and serve.

Warm Char-grilled Mushroom Salad with Roasted Butternut Squash, Crispy Potato Galette and Crème Fraîche and Green Peppercorns

Serves 4

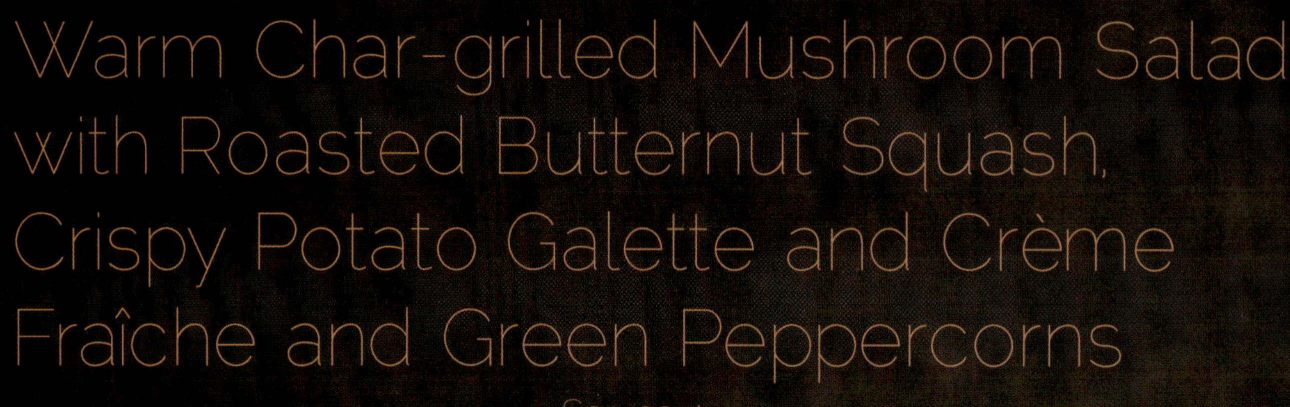

Ingredients

Salad

300 g shitake, oyster and chestnut mushrooms, cleaned
4 large handfuls of baby leaves, well washed
Handful of honey roasted cashews/peanuts
½ red onion, finely sliced
200 g butternut squash, finely sliced; lengthways or crosswise
salt and pepper
1 medium potato (150 g), peeled and coarsely grated lengthways and excess water squeezed out
3 red radishes, finely sliced

Dressing

1 tbsp aged cider vinegar, sherry or white wine vinegar
2 ½ tbsp extra virgin olive oil
scant ½ tsp Dijon mustard
salt to taste
pinch of sugar

Tandoori marinade

1 tsp garlic paste
12 g of ginger made into a paste, strained to get out all the juices
½ tsp red chilli powder
1 tsp salt to taste
¾ tsp garam masala
¾ tsp cumin powder
2 tbsp lemon juice
4 tbsp olive oil

Crème fraîche

6 tbsp crème fraîche
3 scant tsp green peppercorns

- Heat the oven to 180°C.
- Mix together all the ingredients for the tandoori marinade. Keep the small shitake mushrooms and the oyster mushrooms whole, halve the others. Toss them in the marinade making sure each piece is coated; leave for 15-30 minutes.
- Place one layer of butternut squash on a baking tray, lightly oiling and seasoning on both sides. Roast until just soft; around 10-12 minutes. Take out and leave to the side.
- Meanwhile, season the grated potato lightly. Heat 2 tbsp oil in a large non-stick frying pan and taking around a quarter of the mix, place gently in the frying pan in a flat circular form. Repeat with the rest and cook on a gentle flame until golden and crisp on both sides . Remove and place on paper kitchen roll.
- Heat the grill (I use the grill setting of my oven) to high and grill the mushrooms for 8-10 minutes or until lightly charred and cooked through. Give them an occasional stir. (You can place the squash back in the oven to warm through as the mushrooms grill.)
- Whisk together the ingredients for the dressing. Taste and adjust the seasoning and tartness, drizzle a little over the radish.
- Stir together the crème fraîche, peppercorns and a little salt.

To serve

Smear the middle of the plate with crème fraîche, place squash slices on one side but overlapping the crème a little. On the other side arrange the dressed radish slices in a circular flower shape. Toss the baby leaves lightly in the dressing and place in the centre of radish so that you can see the edges. Arrange mushrooms over the leaves and scatter over red onion slices and cashews. Place the fried galette on the side on the leaves, leaning against them, and serve.

Courgette, Basil and Goat Cheese Carbonara

Serves 2

Ingredients

140 g penne or rigatoni pasta
2 tbsp olive oil
½ medium-sized onion, finely sliced
1 fat garlic, chopped finely
1 large courgette, finely sliced
1 egg yolk
80 g goat cheese (weight without the rind)
30 g grated parmesan cheese
6-8 basil leaves, shredded
Good squeeze of lemon juice and ¼ tsp lemon zest
salt and black pepper to taste

- Put a large pot of water to boil. Season with salt and add the pasta, cook until *al dente*.
- Add the oil and garlic to a wide non-stick saucepan or frying pan and heat up gently. Once the garlic has been gently sizzling for 1 minute, add the onions, courgettes, whole basil leaves and a little salt. Stir well to mix, cover, and cook very gently until the courgettes are soft; around 5-7 minutes (depends on thickness of the slice).
- Keeping 3 tbsp of the cooking water drain the pasta and add to the courgettes with the water, and mix well. Turn the heat off, add the goat cheese, shredded basil, parmesan cheese, lemon zest and juice and then the yolk and stir immediately so that the egg coats everything (it will cook in the residual heat). Season to taste with salt and freshly ground black pepper and serve.

Fluffy Spinach Koftas in Creamy Tomato Curry

Serves 4–5

Ingredients

Spinach Koftas

(makes 20 small round koftas)
200 g ricotta cheese
200 g spinach, well washed (I use whole leaf spinach for more flavour)
2 tbsp cornflour

Curry

5 tbsp vegetable oil plus oil for deep frying
1 medium-sized onion, sliced
3 garlic cloves, peeled
10 g ginger, peeled weight
2 large red tomatoes, quartered and deseeded
40 g cashew nuts
600 ml water
2-3 tbsp double cream or a knob of butter (optional)
salt to taste

Spices

½ tsp turmeric powder
¼-½ tsp red chilli powder or ½ tsp paprika powder for colour
1¼ tsp coriander powder
1 tsp cumin powder
1 tsp garam masala powder

- Make a paste of the tomatoes, garlic and ginger.
- Heat the oil in a large non-stick saucepan. Add the onion and cook until lightly browned. Add the tomato paste, cashew nuts, spices and seasoning. Cook over moderate heat, stirring occasionally, until the paste releases oil; around 15 minutes.
- Blend to a fine purée, adding half the water to help. Pour back into the pan and add the remaining water, bring to a boil and simmer until the curry is of a single cream consistency; around 5-8 minutes.
- While the curry is cooking, make the dumplings. Wilt the spinach in a pan with a little water and a pinch of salt. Once cool enough to handle, squeeze out all the excess water and blend to a coarse purée.

Pomegranate Soufflé with Rose and Raspberry Cream

Serves 4

Ingredients

Soufflé

250 ml pomegranate juice
2 tsp (slightly rounded) cornflour
30 g sugar plus 1½ tbsp extra for meringue and some to line the ramekins
2 egg whites
soft butter to brush the ramekins

Rose and raspberry cream

120 g single cream
20 g sugar
2 tsp rose water to taste
150 g raspberries, 100 g kept whole and the rest mashed and strained through a sieve to extract all the juices

- For the soufflé, whisk 25 ml of the pomegranate juice into the cornflour until well amalgamated. Bring the remaining pomegranate juice to a boil and reduce to 125 ml; around 4 minutes. You will need to pour it back into the measuring jug to check (don't worry if it slightly over-reduces).
- Add 30 g of sugar and once it has dissolved whisk in the cornflour slurry (it will start to thicken almost immediately). Bring to a boil, whisking all the while; boil for 1-1½ minutes. Scrape into a container you can blend in (I use the same measuring jug and my stick blender). Set aside to cool.
- Butter the ramekins well and dust the insides with sugar so they are well coated. This is a good time to make the cream. Take 50 g of the berries, mash well and strain through a sieve so you have a seed-free juice. Stir into the cream along with the sugar and rose water. Fold in the whole raspberries and adjust sugar and rose water to taste.
- Heat the oven to 180°C.
- Whisk the egg whites until they reach soft peaks, sprinkle in the extra 1½ tbsp of sugar and continue whisking until the meringue is glossy and firm.
- Blend the jelly so that it is smooth again. Place in a large bowl and whisk in around ¼ of the meringue mix. Then, using a large spoon, carefully fold in the rest, trying to keep the lightness as you incorporate all the little lumps; but do not over mix. Spoon equally into the ramekins and flatten the tops with a palette knife or any other knife. Run the tip of your thumb around the inner rim of the ramekins and place in the oven.
- Bake on the middle shelf for 8-9 minutes or until well risen and slightly golden on the top. Serve immediately with the rose and raspberry cream.

EUROPEAN
I.C.

Ian Curley

Born in Coventry, England, Chef Ian Curley moved to Australia in 1988 after honing his skills in classical cuisine by working in London restaurants. He is the Executive Chef for 7 diverse venues, 5 kitchens and manages a kitchen brigade of over 30 staff. His cooking is often sought out by other industry professionals, both international and local. Ian has prepared meals for many a visiting celebrity, ranging from actors, musicians to sportspersons. Ian has become well known in the industry and beyond for his classical approach to preparing creative meals. He sources the best produce available, focusing on seasonality and presents it simply. Ian is regularly approached by the media for his wealth of knowledge and expertise. He has featured in radio programs and appeared on television shows, including his own reality show, Conviction Kitchen, teaching recently released prison inmates skills to provide them with a new start in life. In keeping with this theme of lending a hand Ian is a passionate supporter of many charities.

Menu 1

Spiced Braised Lamb Shank and White Bean Soup, Mint Yogurt

Beef Wellington with Petit Pois, Foie Gras

Passion Fruit and Citrus Delice

Menu 2

Steak Tartare with Traditional Condiments

Duck Cassoulet with Confit Leg, Fennel and Orange Salad

Banana and Coconut Bombe Alaska, Chocolate Sauce

Menu 3

Duck and Pork Terrine, Condiments, Toasted Baguette

John Dory with Cauliflower Purée and Braised Witlof

Rhubarb and Almond Tart

Menu 4

Tortelloni Roast Pumpkin, Ricotta and Pinenuts

Pan-fried Baby Snapper Fillets, Eggplant Caviar, Squid Ink Taramasalata, Cuttlefish Fricassée

Chocolate Salty Caramel, Peanuts and Sour Cream Ice Cream

Menu 5

Savoury Tart

Pan-fried Sage and Ricotta Gnocchi

Olive Oil Polenta and Ricotta Trifle

WAG
LOPEDIA

Spiced Braised Lamb Shank and White Bean Soup, Mint Yogurt

Serves 25

Ingredients

Soup

500 g cannellini beans
5 litres water
(soak overnight)

- Place the beans in water, bring to a boil, then simmer until they are soft and tender.
- Once they are cooked rinse under cold water then drain. They are now ready for the soup.

Lamb shank braising

5 lamb shanks
salt and pepper to season
5 litres lamb remi or chicken stock
half a carrot
2 sticks of celery
1 onion
1 bay leaf

- Coat lamb shanks in flour and pan-fry until golden brown.
- Place in a large pot with all the roughly chopped vegetables. Add 5 litres of stock, bring to a boil, then simmer gently until lamb shanks are falling away easily from the bone and are tender.
- Strain and use the stock for the lamb shank soup and cool lamb shanks.
- Shred lamb shank meat and mix into the soup.

Chermoula

8 cloves garlic
1½ tsp coriander seeds
1 tsp white peppercorns
½ tsp cinnamon bark
4 tsp cumin seeds
½ tsp ground ginger
(roast and pound the above in mortar pestle)
½ tsp cayenne pepper
2 tsp paprika
½ or 1 tsp saffron, freshly toasted and ground (optional)
1 cup lemon juice
4-6 bullet chillies, chopped fine
1½ tsp salt
10 tsp olive oil
1 cup coriander leaves, chopped
1 cup parsley leaves, chopped
2 onions, finely chopped
(last three optional)

- Mix all the above ingredients for the chermoula sauce.

Lamb shank soup

250 g carrots, small dices
250 g celery, small dices
250 g leeks, small dices
250 g onions, small dices
250 g fennel stalks, small dices
2 ½ cloves of garlic, finely chopped
500 g cannellini beans, cooked
250 g chermoula mix
8 lts of lamb stock
10 braised lamb shanks, shredded

Mint yogurt

250 ml organic natural yogurt
½ bunch mint
lemon juice
salt and pepper to taste

To serve

peas, broad beans runner beans
spinach parsley
mint yogurt, olive dust

- In a large pan, sweat off all the vegetables, season lightly with salt and pepper, add garlic, place the shredded lamb shanks and combine all together.
- Add chermoula mix and cook out the spices.
- Then, use braising lamb stock from the shanks and pour it over the meat and vegetables.
- Add the cannellini beans which are already cooked, season according to taste.
- Add the chopped parsley and coriander in the end.
- When ready to serve, add peas and spinach. You can also serve with the mint yogurt.

EUROPEAN
161 Spring Street, MELBOURNE
Telephone +61 3 9654 0811
LUNCH MENU
APPETISERS
Calamari "Bolognese style" 16.50
Potted Crystal Bay prawns 16.50
Kefalograviera saganaki 11.50
12.00
Smoked fish croquettes 11.50
Marinated olives 9.00
Bruschetta 10.50
Truffled duck liver parfait 18.00
CAVIAR: .... Market $
SHUCKED OYSTERS: with bottarga & horseradish: .. 3.90
& ONION PIZZETTA 13.50
FOIE GRAS (25G): with brioche 23.50
BUFFALO MOZZARELLA (100G) 22.50
IBÉRICO (50G) & sourdough bread 41.00
JAMÓN SERRANO (50G) & sourdough bread 21.50
Spiced braised lamb shank & white bean soup, mint yoghurt .20.50
Duck & pork terrine, condiments & toasted baguette............21.50
Tortelloni of roast pumpkin, ricotta and pinenuts 23.50
Spaghetti alla marinara 23.50/31.50
Seasonal mushroom risotto with truffle oil 21.50/28.00
Confit duck and mushroom pie, mustard & prune sauce 36.50
Whole roast fish, herb salad & vegetable fritter .... Market $
Twice cooked lamb belly, chickpea ragout, imam bayildi........36.50
The European pepper steak 37.50
Cotoletta of free range pork with Italian coleslaw 35.50
Veal Holstein 35.50
Popeseye minute steak with rocket & parmesan 35.50
Handcut French fries 11.00
European chef salad 12.00
Cos lettuce, egg & anchovy10.50
Baby beans & almonds 10.50
DESSERTS
Cheese (50G): served with bread...........................
Chocolate salty caramel, peanuts &

Beef Wellington with Petit Pois, Foie Gras

Serves 10

Ingredients

10 x 160 g eye fillet steak, trimmed of all sinew and fat
10 tsp Dijon mustard
10 x 15 g proscuitto slice
10 x 30 g strip of brioche pastry, 2 cm wide and 15 cm long
10 heaped tablespoon of mushroom duxelles
sea salt
freshly milled white pepper
1 egg yolk beaten with a pinch of salt

Brioche

1.5 kg flour
20 g dry yeast
160 ml milk
20 g salt
90 g sugar
22 eggs
960 g butter

- Combine dry ingredients, add milk and eggs.
- Work for 5 minutes.
- Start adding butter bit by bit.
- Leave it to cool overnight.
- For beef wellington, roll out the cold brioche to 4 mm thickness and cut into strips 3 cm wide by 22 cm long.

- Wrap around the beef, glaze with egg yolk and it is ready to place in the oven.

Mushroom duxelles

3 shallots, finely diced
2 cloves of garlic, finely chopped
1 kg champignons or button mushrooms, finely chopped
5 sprigs of thyme, picked
2 tbsp olive oil
sea salt
freshly milled black pepper

- Heat oil in a heavy bottom pan. Sweat shallots and garlic until soft.
- Add mushrooms and cook until all the liquid has evaporated. Stir regularly with a wooden spoon.
- Add thyme and season. Remove from heat and allow it to cool.

Button mushroom garnish

350 g baby button mushrooms
3 shallots, sliced
garlic oil
350 ml cream
100 ml vegetable nage
3 tbsp red wine sauce
100 g fresh peas
5 baby cos lettuce leaves, cut into julienne
8 baby brussel sprout leaves or asparagus spears (season dependent)
salt and pepper

- Sweat the shallots in the garlic briefly without letting it change colour.
- Add the mushrooms and cook for a minute.
- Add the cream and a little vegetable nage, simmer, then add red wine sauce to give it the colour of café latté.
- Add the peas and cook for a minute, then add the sprout leaves and cook for another minute. Finally add the cos leaves and season.

Mushroom froth

3 shallots, finely sliced
500 g button mushrooms, finely sliced
10 g dry mushrooms (dried cepes/forestiere mix)
3 sprigs of thyme
500 g unsalted butter
100 ml olive oil
1 litre water
100 ml cream
salt and freshly milled black pepper
skimmed milk
foie-gras shavings

- Heat butter and oil in a heavy bottom pan.
- Add shallots and cook until soft.
- To this add the button mushrooms and thyme. Turn up heat and cook until all the moisture has evaporated from the mushrooms.
- Add water and the dried mushrooms, reduce completely to a glaze.
- After adding the cream, return to boil then season.
- Strain and keep liquid. Use mushrooms for another purpose.

Finishing the froth

Add 1 teaspoon skim milk to 2 dessert spoons of mushroom cream, add a pinch of foie-gras shavings and froth with a stick blender.

Pea purée

375 g frozen peas
150 g thickened cream
3 g sea salt
1 g freshly milled black pepper

- Bring cream to a simmer in a wide heavy bottom pan.
- Add the peas and bring back to a simmer quickly.
- Season and remove from the heat.
- Blitz in a high speed blender immediately.
- Spread out on a tray and put in the blast chiller to cool quickly.

Beef wellington

- Heat a heavy bottom pan until very hot. Lightly oil and season the eye fillet.
- Seal the steak for about 1 minute on each side. Remove from heat and place in the blast chiller immediately.
- Once chilled, brush the top of the steak with the mustard, then place the mushroom duxelles on top and smooth to a dome shape.
- Wrap the strip of prosciutto over the top of the mushroom neatly with the ends overlapping at the bottom of the steak, trim off any excess prosciutto.
- Neatly wrap the strip of brioche over the top of the prosciutto with the ends overlapping at the bottom of the steak, trim off any excess.
- Place the wellington in the blast chiller (or fridge) to set.
- Brush the pastry with the egg yolk prior to baking.
- Bake at 180°C for 14 minutes for a medium rare steak.

To serve

Place a tablespoon of pea purée in the centre of a main course plate and form into a circle. Place the button mushroom garnish on top of the purée. Place the wellington beside the garnish. Drizzle the plate with a little red wine and Madeira sauce. Spoon the froth on to the button mushroom garnish. Garnish with 3 sprigs of picked watercress.

RAVENTO
i BLANC
NUMERO
CAVA
M 11-12
PINOT PROJECT

CROQUETTES $12.50
SPAGHETTI & MEATBALLS
RISOTTO OF SMOKED SNAPPER, ZUCCHINI & DILL $22
PAN-FRIED RICOTTA & BLACK OLIVE GNOCCHI $22
w/ SWISS BROWN MUSHROOMS, SILVERBEET & GOATS CHEESE
CHICKEN SCHNITZEL w/ ITALIAN COLESLAW $26
SEARED SALMON NIÇOISE $27.50
(AGED 36 months) $14
& BARLEY
E-EYE $24
& CRESS SALAD
STEAK w/
WINE JUS $28
CASSOLET $20
NOTE: 10% SURCHARGE APPLIES ON SUNDAYS & PUBLIC HOLIDAYS
DESSERTS
BITTER CHOCOLATE FONDANT w/ HAZELNUT GELATO $13.50
WARM STICKY DATE PUDDING w/ BUTTERSCOTCH SAUCE & VANILLA ICE-CREAM
WHITE CHOCOLATE & STRAWBERRY CHEESECAKE $12.50
WARM APP w/ VANILLA GELATO
LEMON ED CREAM $8
CHURROS THURSD OUGHNUTS w/ CHOCOLATE SAUCE

Passion Fruit and Citrus Délice

60 portions

Ingredients

Crunchy base

480 g crumble mix
400 g croquantine (Fointine)
400 g white chocolate

- Mix all the ingredients together.

Crumble mix

150 g butter, cold
150 g brown sugar
150 g flour
150 g raw almonds

- Place everything in a food processor and blitz; then bake till golden.

Joconde biscuit

480 g almond powder
160 g sugar
80 g inverted sugar
800 g eggs
32 g orange zest
480 g egg whites
320 g sugar
240 g butter, melted
160 g flour, sifted

- Beat almond powder, the first quantity of sugar, inverted sugar, eggs and orange zest in a mixer till thick.
- Gently whip egg whites with second quantity of sugar to form soft peaks.
- Gently fold the almond mix with whites.
- Fold in melted butter and then flour.
- Spread out onto trays and bake at 200°C for 5 minutes.

Tropical curd

260 g egg yolk
160 g eggs
180 g sugar
260 ml cream
200 g mango purée
200 g pineapple purée
100 g passion fruit
100 ml lime juice
14 g gelatine leaves
340 g butter

- Warm up all ingredients, except gelatine, and butter to 85°C. Add bloomed gelatine, then the cold butter. Blend with stick blender.

Cream cheese mousse

500 g white chocolate
500 g crème anglaise
20 g gelatine leaves
500 g natural yogurt
500 g cream cheese
500 g whipped cream

- Blitz yogurt and cream cheese together, set aside.
- Make anglaise, add soaked gelatin and strain over white chocolate. Stir to melt.
- Fold anglaise into yogurt mix, then fold in whipped cream.

Crème anglaise

280 ml milk
280 ml cream
50 g sugar
110 g egg yolk

- Boil milk and cream.
- Mix sugar and yolks, before adding to milk and cream mixture.
- Cook at 85°C (low heat).

Citrus gel

300 ml passion fruit
300 ml lime juice
400 ml orange juice
1 litre stock syrup 1:1
3 tbsp agar-agar

Honey popcorn

1 bag lightly salted popcorn
60 g honey
120 g sugar
50 g butter

- First layer crunchy base, then tropical curd and then small layer of mousse.
- Then a layer of sponge, followed by a thin layer of curd. Finish with mousse. Freeze.
- Portion into logs, then glaze with Choco Brilliant White let out with a little sugar syrup.
- Cut logs into portions.
- Garnish with fresh passion fruit, orange segments, clotted cream, citrus gel and honey popcorn.

EUROPEAN
161
PUSH

Steak Tartare with Traditional Condiments

Serves 1

Ingredients

80 g diced dry aged eye fillet of beef (from the Argentines that are aged for a minimum of 4 weeks)
10 g Worcestershire sauce
2 ml red Tabasco sauce (4 shakes of the bottle)
10 g tomato sauce
10 g shallots, diced
5 g cornichons, diced
5 g capers, chopped
20 g Dijon mustard
5 ml lemon juice
5 g chopped parsley
2 ½ g sea salt
10 turns of freshly milled white pepper

To serve

Thinly sliced sourdough loaf – 5 circles cut with an 80 mm cutter then toasted
5 potato crisps, fried
(Nicola potatoes thinly sliced on a mandolin, gently fried until crisp and drained on absorbent paper)
1 egg yolk, raw
5 g egg white, cooked and chopped
5 g egg yolk, cooked and chopped
1 tbsp toasted garlic bread crumbs
1 tbsp parsley, chopped
1 g freshly grated horseradish
extra Dijon mustard
½ lemon wrapped in muslin

Polonaise garnish

This is a mixture of finely chopped (or grated) hardboiled egg white and yolk, finely chopped parsley and crispy breadcrumbs

Crispy breadcrumbs

300 g breadcrumbs
75 ml garlic infused oil
2 tbsp (30 g) chopped parsley
salt and freshly milled white pepper

- Place the breadcrumbs in a dry fry pan and add the garlic oil.
- Place over low heat and gently toast, stirring occasionally, for about 15 minutes or until golden.
- Remove from the heat and season. Allow to cool then toss through the parsley.

Tartare

- In a bowl, combine the eye fillet, Worcestershire sauce, Tabasco sauce and tomato sauce, with the shallots, cornichons, capers, mustard, lemon juice and parsley.
- Mix well and season to taste with salt and pepper.

To serve

Serve on a large round main course plate.

- Brush a strip of Dijon mustard down the centre of the plate.
- Place a 100 mm pastry cutter (or ring) at the top right hand side (1 o'clock) and fill with tartare mix.
- Gently flatten the top of the tartare. Then use an egg to make an indentation in the centre of the tartare and place the egg yolk in it. Remove the pastry cutter.
- Sprinkle the polonaise garnish over the tartare and yolk and grate the horseradish on top.
- Place the muslin lemon at the bottom right (5 o'clock).
- Place the pumpernickel disks (sourdough loaf slices) at the top left hand side (11 o'clock) in a stack.
- Place the potato crisps at the bottom left hand side (7 o'clock) in a stack.

EKCO

Duck Cassoulet with Confit Leg, Fennel and Orange Salad

Serves 4

Ingredients

Tomato fennel sugo

120 g fennel, diced
120 g brown onion, diced
24 ml olive oil
a pinch of saffron threads
40 g tomato paste
24 ml Pernod
360 g x A10 (2.5 kg) whole peeled tomatoes, crushed

- Sweat fennel, onion and saffron in olive oil until soft.
- Add tomato paste and cook.
- Deglaze with Pernod, reduce a little.
- Add crushed tomato and season with salt and freshly milled black pepper.
- Simmer for approximately 2 hours or until it reaches the desired consistency.

Cassoulet beans

200 g haricot (Navy) beans soaked overnight in plenty of water
1 flavour bag
½ bunch thyme
1 head garlic, cut in half
2 tbsp peppercorns
4 bay leaves
400 ml hock stock for cooking beans
1 recipe tomato fennel sugo
240 g (1 smoked hock) picked, cooked, smoked ham hock meat
400 ml vegetable nage or leftover ham hock stock

- Rinse beans and cook them in the ham hock stock with the flavour bag until they are tender. Once cooked, strain the stock from the beans and place the beans in a large pot.
- Add the tomato fennel sugo, the ham hock meat and the nage (or hock stock) to the beans. Place over low heat and bring to a simmer, season and cook until beans are soft.

Confit duck

4 duck marylands
200 g rock salt
4 sprigs of thyme
half a cinnamon quill
1 star anise
1 bay leaf
1 cloves of garlic, peeled
½ an orange, zested
duck fat to cover

- Combine all ingredients except duck fat, rub into duck legs, let sit for 4-5 hours.
- Wash duck legs well, place into a baking tray, cover with duck fat.
- Cook 140°C for 2-3 hours till tender.
- Let cool in the fat or remove and vacuum pack ready for service. Alternatively, after washing duck legs, place in vacuum bags and sous vide for 12 hours at 72°C.

Fennel and orange salad

Small handful rocket leaves
½ fennel, shaved
1 orange, segments
¼ red onion, finely sliced
lemon juice and olive oil for dressing

To garnish (per serving)

1 confit duck leg
2 tbsp cassoulet beans
1 slice cotechino
1 slice toulouse sausage
1 slice boudin blanc
1 bacon lardon
1 tbsp potato salad
orange and fennel salad
1 ramekin Dijon mustard

Banana and Coconut Bombe Alaska, Chocolate Sauce

Serves 12

Ingredients

Banana and coconut ice cream (bombe)

2.6 litre cream
3.6 litre milk
1 litre coconut purée
500 g banana purée
2 vanilla beans
72 yolks
1.2 kg sugar

Bring to a boil the cream, milk, coconut purée, vanilla and half the sugar. Whisk the yolks with the remaining sugar and pour the milk mix over the eggs. Pass the mix through a fine sieve and place back in the pot. Cook over low heat until it thickens. Cool before adding the banana and churning. Once ready, pipe into 6 cm diameter x 3 cm deep mould and blast freeze.

Muscovado sponge

100 g egg yolks
125 g egg whites
80 g muscovado sugar
100 g almond meal
30 g plain flour
80 g chopped walnuts

- Whisk yolks till thick.
- Whisk whites to soft peak and fold through whisked egg yolks.
- Combine Muscovado, almond meal and plain flour and strain through a sieve.
- Gently fold dry ingredients into the whipped yolks and whites mixture; a third at a time. Pour batter into a greaseproof paper-lined tray (30 cm x 40 cm), spread to an even thickness.
- Sprinkle chopped walnuts over the top.
- Bake at 160°C for 10 minutes and let it cool.
- Cut out 12 circles with a 7 cm diameter cutter.

Chocolate sauce

340 ml water
150 g sugar
40 g cocoa powder
360 g dark chocolate (72% Michel Cluizel, Kayambe Noir)

- Combine all ingredients in a heatproof bowl and place on a pot of simmering water, stir till molten and smooth. Let this cool.

Italian meringue

200 g egg white
400 g sugar
200 g water

- Bring sugar and water to a boil. Whip egg whites to a soft peak, slowly pour boiling sugar into egg whites with machine still running, keep whipping till cool.
- Time the whipping of the egg whites and the boiling of the sugar to be ready at the same time.

Assembling the bombe

- Place bombe on the cut sponge disks.
- Pipe meringue on bombe using a #7 plain piping nozzle, to look like a porcupine. Place back in blast chiller.

To serve

Place bombe in oven at 180°C for 2 minutes (to soften the ice cream), then blow torch to colour meringue. Slice banana, sprinkle with sugar and gratinate to caramelise. Arrange banana and fresh toasted coconut on the plate. Place baked bombe on the plate. Serve with chocolate sauce on the side.

Duck and Pork Terrine, Condiments, Toasted Baguette

4 Terrines

Ingredients

3 size 25 ducks, boned and diced
1.2 kg veal, mince
1.2 kg pork, mince
500 g pork fat, mince
400 g duck livers
250 g pistachio kernels
2 tbsp green peppercorns
800 ml cream
2 tbsp 5-spice powder
1 tbsp allspice
1 tbsp ground cloves
a pinch of nutmeg
50 g sea salt
50 g freshly milled black pepper
1 kg pitted prunes soaked in hot port
2.5 kg streaky bacon
drizzle of extra virgin olive oil (EVOO)

- Bone ducks and cut meat into large dice (2.5 cm).
- Mix duck meat with remaining ingredients in a large stainless steel bowl. Add some more cream if farce is too stiff.
- Cook a small amount of the farce and check the seasonings, adjust accordingly.
- Line 4 terrine moulds with cling film, then streaky bacon, allowing enough bacon to overlap and completely encase the terrine.
- Half fill the moulds with farce, place a line of prunes in the centre and add the remaining farce to overlap the bacon. Then overlap the cling film and wrap the tops of the terrines with foil.
- Place in bain-maries and cook for 20 minutes at 160°C, then drop the temperature to 140°C and continue to cook for another 20-25 minutes. When the core temperature is 57-58°C they are cooked sufficiently.
- Remove terrines from bain-maries and allow to cool to room temperature on a wire rack . Then place weights on top of them and put them into the coolroom overnight.
- Once the terrines are pressed, they should then be removed from the terrine moulds, wiped clean (with paper), then cryovac-packed and dated.
- The terrine is sliced 1 cm thick (140 g portion) and rubbed with a drizzle of EVOO and topped with a pinch of flaked sea salt.
- It is served on a main course plate with a salad of herbs, capers, pickled carrot purée, sliced pickled onion and sliced pickled cucumber, dressed with EVOO. Also 1 tbsp piccalilli, 1 slice (long) toasted sourdough baguette brushed with oil.

Pickled carrot purée

2 carrots, diced
200 ml muscatel vinaigrette reduction
bay leaf and thyme
2 tbsp honey
2 tbsp butter

- Vacuum pack carrots, vinegar and herbs, place in sous vide till tender. Blitz in jug blender, adding the butter, honey and seasoning till smooth and glossy.

Pickled carrots

sliced baby heirloom carrots
1 cinnamon stick
2 star anise
4-5 cloves
Muscatel vinaigrette reduction (house dressing)

- Combine all ingredients, bring to a simmer, turn off. Let it cool, vacuum pack and use when required.

Pickled cucumber

- Cut cucumber into cubes, vacuum pack with muscatel vinaigrette reduction.

Port-soaked currents

- Heat port, pour over currents, cool, use as required.

PRINCES

John Dory with Cauliflower Purée and Braised Witlof

Serves 4

Ingredients

72 g John Dory fillets per person

Purée

1 cauliflower (slice one third and set the rest aside for later)
100 ml milk
salt and pepper

- Heat milk to a boil and drop in ⅔ cauliflower and cook until tender.
- Strain but keep liquid to adjust consistency of purée.
- Blend cauliflower in a jug blender until very smooth and adjust with liquid so purée is silky.
- Season and keep warm.

Confit fennel

1 medium fennel, de-cored and diced
enough olive oil to cover
1 orange, zested
1 segment of orange, finely diced
a pinch of salt

- Dice fennel and cover with oil in pot or deep tray.
- Place on low heat on stove and cook (not boil) until tender.
- Remove and add zest and segment of orange and season with salt.

Braised witlof

3 witlof
1 litre chicken stock
5 oranges (2 zested, 3 juiced)
¼ bunch thyme
1 bay leaf
40 g butter
salt and pepper

- Cut witlof in ¼" pieces lengthways.
- Place in deep tray or pot with all ingredients, bring to a simmer and cover with foil.
- Cook until tender on low heat in the oven or on the stove until tender. Remove from liquid and seal in a hot pan or grill just before you serve.

Cauliflower 'confetti'

remaining ⅓ cauliflower cut into small florets
olive oil
salt and pepper

- Season and coat cauliflower in oil and bake in a moderate heated oven until well-coloured and tender.

Curry oil

1 tsp curry powder
44 ml vegetable oil
1 clove
½ cinnamon stick
salt

- Infuse all ingredients in oil and then strain.

To serve

Spoon cauliflower purée in the centre of the plate and top with grilled witlof. Sprinkle around the roasted cauliflower florets, dried Muscatel grapes, pine nuts, orange and fennel confit. Place fish on top, garnish with microherbs and a little curry oil.

Rhubarb and Almond Tart

12 portions

Ingredients

Sweet pastry

500 g icing sugar
1 kg butter
100 ml milk
3 eggs
1.750 kg flour

In the food processor, using the paddle attachment, cream the butter and icing sugar together. Then add the egg and milk; a little at a time. Add the flour and mix until just combined. Remove from food processor and finish by hand. Let it rest before use.

Frangipani

500 g butter
500 g sugar
8 eggs
50 g flour
500 g almond meal

Cream butter and sugar, add the eggs one at a time. Add the flour and almond meal and mix well.

Poached rhubarb

800 g rhubarb
150 g sugar

Syrup

700 g sugar
375 g sweet wine
2 old vanilla beans
1 litre water
1 cinnamon stick
2 oranges, zested

Wash, peel and cut the rhubarb, then roll in sugar. Let it stand for half an hour. Bring the syrup up to a boil with the rhubarb skins, cook for 10 minutes, remove the skins Place the rhubarb in and simmer it slowly (it does not take long). You want it to hold its shape when its cooked.

To assemble

- Line flan tin with sweet pastry. Blind bake and let it cool.
- Spread a thin layer of rhubarb on the base of the pastry, pipe/spread frangipani over the top to fill the flan.
- Top with pieces of poached rhubarb and sprinkle on slivered almonds.
- Bake at 160°C till cooked; approx 35 minutes.

Tortelloni of Pumpkin and Ricotta

15 portions

Ingredients

1.8 kg butternut pumpkin
(roasted/skinned/deseeded/hung)
1 kg ricotta, hung overnight
500 g smoked Scamorza, diced
200 g cavolo nero (black cabbage)
50 g baby spinach
360 g pine nuts, toasted
2 small nutmegs, grated
sea salt
freshly milled black pepper

- Roast pumpkin until soft and well cooked. Remove from oven and allow it to cool.
- Skin and deseed the pumpkin, hang the pulp for 24 hours in a muslin bag or filter paper. Keep the drained juice. Reduce the liquid to a glaze, reserve to use later.
- Wilt cavolo nero and spinach in olive oil and season. Cool and squeeze out as much water as possible.
- Combine pumpkin, ricotta, Scarmoza, cavolo nero, spinach and pine nuts and mix well. Season to taste.

Pasta dough

3 eggs
8 egg yolks
550 g OO Flour or baker's flour-strong high gluten flour
½ tsp extra virgin olive oil (EVOO)
½ tsp fine sea salt

- Roll dough out thinly, cut disk with a 10 cm cutter.
- Spoon 2 tbsp of filling onto the centre, brush a little egg wash on pasta and fold in half to seal. Bring the two edges together to make tortelloni and cook when required.

Jacqueline sauce

1 cinnamon stick
5 carrots, grated
1 knob ginger, sliced
10 coriander seeds
5 cardamom pods
5 star anise
2 cloves
400 ml vermouth
1 litre chicken stock
500 g butter
50 ml vegetable oil

- Sweat ginger and spices in butter and oil until fragrant. Add carrot and boil for 10 minutes.
- Add vermouth, chicken stock and butter and cook for 10 minutes. Strain through fine strainer.
- Return to pot and reduce for 15 minutes.

Garnishes

50 ml jacqueline sauce
2 amaretti biscuits
2 g chopped chives
10 g diced mustard fruits

- Add 1 cardamom pod, 1 clove, 1 star anise, ¼ of the jacqueline base, reduce and add 100 ml cream. Blitz.

Tortelloni salad

20 g herb salad with popcorn shoots (if available)
15 g candied pine nuts/pumpkin seeds
20 g herb salad
15 g crispy pumpkin
5 ml white balsamic vinegar
5 ml EVOO
1-2 turns of peppermill and 1 pinch salt

To serve

Blanch tortelloni till cooked. Heat pan with butter. Once foaming, add sage leaves and tortelloni, fry till slightly crisp. Serve with jaqueline sauce, crushed amaretti biscuits, mustard fruits and cress. Drizzle a bit of the pumpkin glaze over the rotolo.

Pan-fried Baby Snapper Fillets, Eggplant Caviar, Squid Ink Taramasalata, Cuttlefish Fricassée

Serves 4

Ingredients

150 g baby snapper fillet, pin-boned
1 Morton bay bug meat (or lobster/langoustine), sliced
1 baby calamari body, sliced fine
50 g shaved baby fennel
basil leaves
diced cuts of snapper
red vein sorrel leaves
blanched citrus zest
bottarga or air-dried tuna

Eggplant caviar

2 eggplants
1 tsp sliced garlic
thyme
salt and pepper
extra virgin olive oil (EVOO)

- Cut eggplant in half score, place sliced garlic and thyme, season, put the two halves together, wrap in foil and bake till soft.
- Scrape out flesh, mash with fork and season.

Tomato compote

1 small red pepper
2 tomatoes
1 tbsp extra virgin olive oil
¼ large red onion, finely dice
1 clove of garlic
a pinch of brown sugar
13 ml sherry
13 ml sherry vinegar
1 bullet chilli, deseeded

- Peel the red pepper, cut into 5 mm dices. Peel and deseed tomato and cut into rough 5 mm dices.
- Sauté onion and red pepper in olive oil, with a pinch of salt and pepper, till soft.
- Add garlic and cook for a minute. Add sherry and sherry vinegar. Add the tomato and cook gently for 20 minutes until rich and excess liquid has gone. Add sugar and season to taste.

Squid ink taramasalata

20 g tarama paste
1 slice thick white bread or ⅛ Turkish bread
1 clove garlic, crushed
a squeeze of lemon
50 ml vegetable oil
250 ml olive oil
approx. 100 ml ice cold water
a drop of squid ink

- Soak bread in water and squeeze out the excess.
- Purée garlic, bread and tarama in a processor until smooth. Add lemon juice and then the oils. Use iced water to let down the mix if it gets too thick.
- Check seasoning. Add more lemon juice if too salty.
- Place in suitable container (preferably a plastic bucket with a sealable lid). Allow it to sit in the refrigerator for at least 30 minutes so that the flavours can combine.

To serve

Pan-fry seasoned snapper fillet skin side down to crisp the skin, flip over and top with citrus zest and bottarga. Sauté shaved fennel, add fish dices, cook, add eggplant caviar, warm tomato compote and the basil leaves. Sauté bug meat and calamari, season.

To plate

Spoon eggplant caviar mixture in the centre of the plate. Top with sautéed calamari and bug meat. Dot tarama around the centre. Top with snapper. Garnish with red vein sorrel leaves, basil oil and bottarga.

Chocolate Salty Caramel, Peanuts and Sour Cream Ice Cream

25 pieces

Ingredients

Salty caramel

500 g sugar
enough water to just wet sugar
300 ml clotted cream
100 g butter
15 g fleur de sel salt (sea salt)

- Make a caramel with the sugar and water.
- Break the caramel with the cream and salt.
- Set in containers.

Crumbled peanut base

250 g peanuts roasted
4 g salt
200 g milk chocolate melted
250 g hazelnut praliné paste
125 g fointine

- Blitz nuts and salt in food processor. Mix melted chocolate and hazelnut praliné paste. Mix all ingredients together. Spread on a tray to crumble.

Chocolate mousse

200 g cream
40 g egg yolk
20 g sugar
90 g Maralumi, 64% dark chocolate

- Boil cream and sugar and pour over yolks. Return to stove and cook out for one minute. Strain over chocolate while still hot, mix together. Pour into piping bags.

To serve

Pipe small amounts of mousse in half-sphere moulds. Use a spoon and push up the sides, allowing room for the crumbled peanut base and salty caramel inside. Using a palette knife, close with more mousse until flush and set in blast chiller. When cold join two half-spheres with a tiny amount of mousse and rub the joint so it becomes smooth.

For coating

200 g Maralumi, 64% dark chocolate
200 g cocoa butter

- Melt over double boiler, dip and sprinkle with fleur de sal salt (tiny amount) and chill.

Sour cream sorbet

500 ml sour cream
250 ml milk
½ tsp stabiliser
275 g sugar
275 ml water
21lime zest
¼ stalk lemongrass
1½ teaspoons glucose
½ vanilla bean
50 ml orange-flavoured brandy liqueur

- Mix all ingredients except for sour cream and milk together in a pot and bring to boil. Cool and add sour cream and milk. Sieve and churn.

Chocolate sauce

450 ml water
450 g sugar
270 g dark chocolate
40 g cocoa powder
45 g glucose
30 g corn starch

- In a large pot add water, sugar, chocolate, cocoa and glucose. Bring to a boil, stirring constantly.
- Add cornstarch (mixed with water) and bring back to a boil. Pass into a fine sieve.

Caramelised peanuts

250 g raw unsalted peanuts
150 g sugar
75 ml water
cocoa powder
edible gold dust

- Heat sugar and water to 121°C. Add peanuts and stir until mixture crystallises and turns into caramel. Tip onto baking sheet and let it cool.
- Take half these nuts, roll in melted dark chocolate and coat modestly in cocoa and then in gold dust.

Peanut brittle

58 g sugar
170 g glucose
125 ml water
¼ teaspoon salt
150 g unsalted peanuts chopped
1 tbsp butter
1 tsp bicarb

- Heat sugar, water and glucose to 121°C (mild heat).
- Add salt and peanuts and cook to 143°C. Mix in butter and bicarb and then tip onto baking sheet to cool.

Chocolate shard (24 shards)

175 g melted compound chocolate
50 g caramelised peanuts (roughly chopped)

- Using a palette knife, spread melted chocolate over a baking sheet and sprinkle with chopped nuts. Wait to set and neaten edges so they are straight.. With a knife, cut 12 x 1 cm strips.
- Store in an airtight container with layers of greaseproof paper in between each layer.

To serve

Place crushed caramel peanuts on the plate, top with choc salty ball and a ball of sour cream sorbet. Sprinkle around some caramelised peanuts, top with chocolate shards and grate over peanut brittle.

SHOVELTON & STOREY
PRINTERS

THE
MELBOURNE
SUPPER CLUB
Sparkling
NV Clover Hill Tasmanian Cuvée
NV Doyard Vendemiaire Brut Blanc de Blancs
White

Savoury Tart

Serves 5

Ingredients

Pâte brisée

(savoury pastry)

1 kg flour
600 g butter
4 eggs
a pinch of salt
a pinch of sugar
0.12 litre milk

- In a large bowl, rub flour, salt, sugar and butter till it looks like large bread crumbs. Add egg and milk and mix until combined. Divide into 5 even balls and chill.

Savoury custard

100 g crème fraîche
700 g cream
150 g milk
4 eggs
4 yolks
salt and pepper

- Whisk all ingredients together. Fill blind-baked pastry case with favourite filling and pour custard on top.
- Top with cheese if desired. Bake at 160°C till set.

Pan-fried Sage and Ricotta Gnocchi

Serves 7

Ingredients

1.1 kg baked desirée potatoes
30 g Parmesan, finely grated
½ bunch sage, finely chopped
2 lemons, zested
400-480 g plain flour
1 whole egg
zucchini
fresh peas
broad beans
chives
olive oil

- Cut potatoes in half while still hot and squeeze into a food strainer/crusher.
- Add chives and lemon zests to potato, and gently incorporate the flour. Try not to overwork the dough.
- Gently roll or press dough and cut into required size.
- Blanch gnocchi (the potatoes) in a large pot of boiling seasoned water.
- As soon as the gnocchi rises to the surface carefully lift them into iced water to refresh them.
- Drain the gnocchi and toss in oil, then divide into 180 g portions in plastic containers.

To serve

Pan-fry gnocchi and sauté zucchini in olive oil. Add fresh peas, broad beans, lemon zest and fresh mint. Dust with olive oil and place torn mozzarella on top.

Olive Oil Polenta and Ricotta Trifle

Serves 5

Ingredients

Olive oil polenta cake

6 eggs
440 g sugar
160 ml reserved Hojiblanca olive oil
4 lemons zested and juiced
2 tsp vanilla
380 g polenta
150 g flour
3 tsp baking powder
1 tsp salt

- Whisk eggs and sugar.
- Slowly add olive oil.
- Combine dry ingredients, mix into eggs alternately with lemon juice.
- Bake at 160°C for 40 minutes or until golden brown and cooked.

Ricotta mousse

500 g ricotta (whey cheese)
1 vanilla bean
55 g egg whites
65 g sugar
1 g salt
220 g crème fraîche
100 g cream
2 gelatine leaves

- Blend ricotta and vanilla bean in blender.
- Place in a bowl, fold in crème fraîche.
- Whisk whites to soft peaks, add sugar and salt.
- Fold into cream mixture.
- Warm cream and soaked gelatine leaves, fold into mixture.
- Place into piping bags.

To assemble

- Layer 4 even layers of cake and mousse.
- The cake can be cut into slices or diced, whatever is best for your moulds.
- Garnish with extra Hojiblanca olive oil so it trickles down the layers of the dessert.

Vineet Bhatia

The immensely talented Vineet Bhatia is the owner of Rasoi, a much-visited Indian restaurant in London. He was the first Indian chef-restaurateur in 102 years to receive a Michelin Star when he was awarded one in 2001. He also has the honour of being the only Indian chef to hold two Stars. Rasoi has been awarded the much-coveted Star every year since 2006 while Rasoi by Vineet, in Geneva, Switzerland, has also got the distinction of earning Michelin Stars every year since 2009.

Recipes

Aubergine Chutney, Uttapam Lasagne with Sambhar Peas and Tomato-Coconut Chutney

Banana Leaf-wrapped Baked Sea Bass with Mustard

French Beans-Barley Soup, Tempered Barley-Peanut Masala

Spinach-Cheese and Potato Nests

Grilled Cheesy Lamb Chops, Curry Leaf-tossed Potatoes, Spiced Lamb Jus

Pumpkin-Cinnamon Phirni

Choco Rabdi

Aubergine Chutney, Uttapam Lasagne with Sambhar Peas and Tomato-Coconut Chutney

Serves 4

Ingredients

Uttapam

90 g Basmati rice
30 g urad daal
½ tsp fenugreek seeds
vegetable oil for shallow-frying
salt to taste

- Put the rice, urad daal and fenugreek seeds in a bowl, add enough cold water to cover by 1 cm and leave overnight. The next day, grind the mixture with some salt to a smooth paste in a food processor; adding a little water if it seems too dry to form a paste.
- Heat a little oil in a non-stick frying pan and pour in two tablespoons of the mixture to form pancakes around 5 cm in diameter–you will need 12 altogether. Cook over low to medium heat for about 2 minutes on each side, until set and lightly browned.

Aubergine-sesame chutney

1 aubergine, cut into 1 cm dices
2 spring onions, finely chopped
1 tomato, deseeded and finely chopped
3 tbsp onion and tomato masala
½ tbsp jaggery
2 tbsp sesame seeds, roasted
1 tbsp lemon juice
½ tsp red chilli powder
1 tsp chaat masala
1½ tbsp fresh coriander, finely chopped
vegetable oil for deep-frying
salt to taste

- Heat the vegetable oil to 175°C (moderately) in a deep-fat fryer or a deep saucepan. Add the diced aubergine and fry for 2 minutes or until softened. Drain on kitchen paper and leave to cool.
- Heat the onion-tomato masala in a pan and add the jaggery sesame seeds and red chilli powder, reduce and cook on low heat till the jaggery melts.
- Remove from the heat, cool the mixture and add the fried aubergines, chaat masala, coriander leaves, lemon juice and salt. Set aside.

Sambhar

250 g arhar daal
1½ tsp turmeric
2 tbsp vegetable oil
1 tsp mustard seeds
½ tbsp fresh ginger, chopped
1 sprig of curry leaves
a pinch of asafoetida (optional)
¼ teaspoon fenugreek seeds
1 shallot, chopped
1 tomato, chopped
½ teaspoon red chilli powder
5 cm drumstick (optional)
½ tbsp sambhar powder
1 tbsp tamarind pulp
6 tbsp green peas
1 tbsp fresh coriander roots, chopped

- Place the arhar daal, 1 tsp of the turmeric and some salt in a pan, add four times its volume of water and bring to a boil. Reduce the heat, cover and simmer until tender.
- Heat the oil in a separate pan and add the mustard seeds, ginger, curry leaves and asafoetida (optional).

Once the seeds start to crackle, add the fenugreek seeds, shallot, tomato, chilli powder, drumstick (optional), sambhar powder and the remaining turmeric.

- Pour this tempering over the daal and stir it in, then add the tamarind pulp, green peas and chopped coriander roots. Bring back to a boil and then serve.

Tomato-coconut chutney

1½ tbsp vegetable oil
1 tsp black mustard seeds
1 tsp finely chopped fresh ginger
1 tsp green chillies, finely chopped
10 curry leaves
¾ tsp red chilli powder
A pinch of asafoetida
250 g tomatoes, skinned and chopped
4 tbsp coconut, grated
1 tsp sugar
1 tbsp fresh coriander leaves, finely chopped
salt to taste

- Heat the oil in a pan and add the mustard seeds. As they splutter, add the ginger and green chilli and sauté for a minute.
- Add the curry leaves, chilli powder and asafoetida. Cook for 30 seconds, stir in the chopped tomatoes, sugar and some salt.
- Simmer until the chutney has thickened, then remove from the heat, stir in the grated coconut and leave to cool. Finally, stir in the chopped coriander.

To serve

Sandwich the aubergine chutney between the 3 uttapams to form a portion and serve with sambhar, aubergine-sesame chutney and tomato coconut chutney.

A
B
The Royal Borough of Kensington
and Chelsea
LINCOLN
STREET, S.W.3

Banana Leaf-wrapped Baked Sea Bass with Mustard

Serves 4

Ingredients

4 sea bass fillets, scaled and pin-boned
6 tbsp thick yogurt (Greek yogurt if available)
1 tsp turmeric powder
1 tsp red chilli powder
2 tbsp ginger-garlic paste
3 tbsp grainy mustard paste
1 tbsp vegetable oil
sea salt to taste
½ a lemon, juice
4 slices of lemon
4 banana leaf sheets, 7" x 3"

- Pre-heat oven at 170°C.
- In a bowl add the yogurt, turmeric powder, red chilli powder, ginger-garlic paste, grainy mustard, vegetable oil and salt. Mix together to form a marinade.
- Place the fish in the marinade and leave for at least six hours for the flavours to infuse into the fish.
- Wrap the fish fillet, topped with a slice of lemon in the banana leaf and bake for 6-8 minutes or till the fish is cooked.

Note

Any flat fish could be substituted instead of sea bass.

French Beans-Barley Soup, Tempered Barley-Peanut Masala

Serves 4

Ingredients

French beans-barley soup

2 tbsp vegetable oil
1 tsp cumin seeds
1 tsp garlic, finely chopped
1 tsp green chillies, finely chopped
1 tsp fresh ginger, finely chopped
½ shallot, sliced
200 g beans, chopped
200 ml vegetable stock
6 tbsp single cream
1 bunch of coriander leaves, chopped
½ tsp garam masala
1 tbsp unsalted butter
80 g barley, boiled
salt to taste

- Heat the vegetable oil in a pan and add the cumin seeds. As they begin to splutter, add the garlic, green chillies, ginger and shallot and sauté for 2 minutes until they soften, but do not change colour. Add the French beans and sauté for 2 minutes, then pour in the vegetable stock and cream. Bring to a boil and add the coriander leaves, garam masala and salt. Stir well and remove from the heat. Do not cook the coriander leaves.
- Immediately blitz the soup with a hand blender until smooth and strain through a fine sieve. Add the boiled barley, reheat gently and adjust the seasoning.
- Mix in the butter just before serving.

Tempered barley-peanut masala

2 tbsp butter
1 tsp garlic, chopped
2 tbsp peanuts, chopped
4 tbsp barley, boiled
1 tsp cumin seeds, lightly toasted in a pan
and crushed salt to taste

- Heat butter in a pan and sauté the garlic till it turns light golden. Add the chopped peanuts and sauté for another 2 minutes and add the boiled barley and roasted cumin seeds.
- Remove the pan from the heat and spoon the barley mixture into the soup plate and pour the soup on it. Serve hot.

Spinach-Cheese and Potato Nests

Serves 4

Ingredients

4 large waxy potatoes
2 tsp salt
½ tsp pepper
2½ tsp garlic powder
2½ tsp onion powder
4 tsp vegetable oil
cooking spray
4 cups of frozen spinach, thawed (yields 2 cups cooked)
4 tbsp extra virgin olive oil
4 large eggs

- Preheat oven at 180°C.
- Grate the potatoes, add 1 tsp of salt, mix well and let this sit in a colander with a bowl under it for 20 minutes.
- In a large skillet, sauté spinach in olive oil. Season with 2 tsp garlic powder, 2 tsp onion powder and 1 tsp salt. Cook until most of the water had evaporated, which should be for 6-8 minutes. Set aside.
- Squeeze as much water out of the grated potatoes as you can. Season with ½ tsp garlic powder, ½ tsp onion powder and ½ tsp pepper. Add 4 tsp vegetable oil and mix well.
- Generously spray a 12 muffin tin pan with cooking spray.
- Arrange grated potatoes into each muffin cup, pressing against the bottom and up the sides.
- Place this in the oven for 15 minutes or until they start to brown slightly. Remove from the oven and set aside.
- Beat eggs in a medium-sized bowl, add a pinch of salt and spinach and mix until well combined.
- Evenly spoon spinach in each potato nest. Sprinkle grated mozzarella or cheddar. Bake for 10 minutes or until the egg is cooked. Remove from the oven and let these cool slightly.
- Carefully unmould each potato nest using a butter knife around the edges of the nest.

Grilled Cheesy Lamb Chops, Curry Leaf-tossed Potatoes, Spiced Lamb Jus

Serves 4

Ingredients

Lamb chops

8 two-bone lamb chops, fat removed, lightly pricked with the tip of a knife

Marinade

3 tbsp vegetable oil
1 tbsp ginger-garlic paste
1 tsp ginger, chopped
1 tsp garlic, chopped
½ tsp red chilli powder
½ tbsp fresh red chilli-garlic paste
½ tsp garam masala powder
½ lemon, juice
1 tbsp coriander stems, chopped
Sea salt to taste

Cheese topping

6 tbsp grated cheddar cheese
2 tbsp grated mozzarella
1 tbsp coriander stems chopped
½ tsp red chilli powder
½ teaspoon garam masala powder

- Mix together all the ingredients and rub onto the lamb chops and keep aside for at least 6 hours for the flavours to get absorbed into the lamb.
- Heat a heavy bottomed pan or a non stick pan and place the lamb chops in it. Sear the outsides all around for a minute.
- Transfer to a roasting tray and top the chops with the cheese mixture and place under a hot grill for a couple of minutes till the cheese melts.

Curry leaf-tossed potatoes

2 tbsp vegetable oil
1 tbsp black mustard seeds
½ tbsp garlic, chopped
½ tbsp ginger, chopped
1 tsp green chilli, chopped
1 small white onion, sliced
10 curry leaves
½ tsp turmeric powder
½ tsp red chilli powder
3 large potatoes (boiled in water with a garlic clove, salt, a pinch each of turmeric and red chilli powder, cooled, peeled and cut into ½ inch cubes)
½ lemon juice
sea salt to taste

- Heat oil in a pan and add black mustard seeds. As they begin to splutter add chopped garlic, ginger and green chilli.
- Sauté for 1 minute and add the sliced onions and curry leaves. Sweat the onions till pink and add the turmeric and red chilli powder, toss for one minute and add the boiled diced potatoes.
- Gently toss the potatoes and sprinkle the sea salt and lemon juice. Mix together.

Spiced lamb jus

1 tbsp vegetable oil
2 green cardamom pods
½ tsp cumin seeds
½ tsp black peppercorns
1 small blade of mace
1 small bay leaf
1 tsp garlic, chopped
1 tsp fresh ginger, chopped
1 tsp chopped green chillies
2 tbsp onion and tomato masala
50 g lamb trimmings
200 ml lamb stock
8-10 mint leaves
salt to taste

- Heat the oil in a pan and add the whole spices, bay leaf, garlic, ginger and green chillies. Sauté for a minute, then add the onion and tomato masala and sauté for two minutes longer. Add the lamb trimmings and raise the heat and cook until seared.
- Pour in the lamb stock. Bring to a boil, reduce the heat to a simmer and add the mint stalks and some salt. Cook gently for 10 minutes, remove from the heat and leave to infuse for 5 minutes.
- Strain through a fine sieve and check the seasoning.

Pumpkin Cinnamon Phirni

Serves 4

INGREDIENTS

2 tbsp ghee
1 tsp cardamom seeds, crushed
2 tbsp almonds, chopped
1 tbsp pine nuts
2 tbsp pistachio, chopped
2 tbsp raisins
2-3 cups of pumpkin purée, boiled
½ tsp cinnamon powder
2 cups milk
2-3 cups of rice, boiled
½ cup cream
3 tbsp sugar
3 tbsp white chocolate

- In a heavy bottomed pot heat the ghee and add the crushed cardamom pods, almonds, pine nuts, pistachio and raisins; toast them lightly. Follow this with the pumpkin purée and cinnamon powder.
- Spoon in the boiled rice to the mixture. Pour in milk, cream and white chocolate and cook till mixture thickens.
- Pour in moulds to set.

Choco Rabdi

Serves 4

INGREDIENTS

400 ml milk
250 ml cream
25 gm sugar
1 tbsp cocoa powder
2 tbsp dark chocolate, grated
a pinch of green cardamom powder

- In a heavy bottomed pan bring the milk and cream to a boil, lower the heat and reduce the mixture to about 150 ml, while stirring it continuously to prevent it from burning.
- Add sugar, dark chocolate and cocoa powder to the reduced milk. Whisk it till smooth and cool. Add the green cardamom powder. This mixture should have a thick consistency. Keep aside. Serve when cool.

Junoon
Vikas Kha

Vikas Khanna

Inspired by his roots in Amritsar, Punjab, Vikas Khanna has been making waves in world cuisine for a while now. In 2011, he was given the Rising Star Chef Award by Star Chefs for his role in shaping the future of American cuisine. His restaurant Junoon, in New York, was awarded a Star by the Michelin Guide in 2012 and 2013. He also received a proclamation from the New York City Council for his outstanding contribution to the city, and was chosen New Yorker of the Week by NY1. He is a prominent face on cooking shows, having appeared on Gordon Ramsay's Hell's Kitchen and Kitchen Nightmares. He hosted the second and third seasons of MasterChef India and is currently hosting Junior MasterChef.

Kodak
Kodak
ARGENT
TO SOUTHBOUND
7 AVE
TURN HERE
ONE WAY
W 45 ST
GEORGE ABBOTT
NOVOTEL
MARQUIS
Marriott
MARQUIS
BOX OFFICE

Menu 1

5 COURSE SEAFOOD TASTING

Lotus Root Three Ways

Puréed, fried and pickled

Octopus Chaat

Confit octopus, baby heirloom tomatoes, tamarind gel

Red Snapper and Moley Foam

Seared red snapper with moley foam

Kerala Crab Curry

Deep-fried soft shell crab, coconut and smoked kokum curry sauce

Saffron Panna Cotta

Yogurt and lime sorbet

Menu 2

7 COURSE TASTING MENU

Watermelon Shorba

Kaffir lime and ginger, coriander oil, green chili basil seeds

Lahsooni Gobi

Fried cauliflower, tomato garlic chutney

Tandoori Quail

Red current marinated quail, sautéed swiss chard, yellow daal

Bagara Baingan

Baby eggplants simmered in tamarind peanut sauce

Masaledaar Lamb Chops

Tandoori lamb chops with brown butter pomegranate sauce and curry confit potatoes

Saag Paneer

Cottage cheese gnocchi with spinach purée

Falooda

Rose semifreddo, lime granita

Lotus Root Three Ways

Serves 2

Ingredients

Puréed

225 ml heavy cream
225 ml milk
600 g peeled chopped lotus root
2 g cardamom seed
1 g garam masala
salt to taste

- Simmer all ingredients for about 40 minutes.
- Spin in the blender and pass through a fine chinois. Add salt to taste.

Fried

2–3 lotus roots

- Peel and slice 2–3 lotus roots very thinly on a mandolin, to less than ⅛ of an inch.
- Rinse in cold water and dry off.
- Deep-fry at 150°C until golden brown

Pickled

230 ml water
230 ml white vinegar
230 ml rice wine vinegar
2 g black cardamom
2 g Omani lemon
2 g roasted cumin
2 g roasted coriander seeds
200 g palm sugar
2–3 lotus roots
salt to taste

- Mix all the spices together with the vinegars, water, palm sugar and salt.
- Simmer for 30 minutes and strain.
- Peel and slice the lotus root paper-thin and cook the slices in boiling water for 2–3 minutes.
- Add to the hot pickling liquid. Let sit for 24 hours before using.

Octopus Chaat

Serves 4-6

Ingredients

Confit octopus

550 g cumin
550 g coriander seeds
225 g whole red chillies
120 g black cardamom
550 g garlic
225 g deghi mirch
120 g garam masala
7.5 litres canola oil
8 pieces medium-sized octopus

- Fry the cumin and black cardamom in two cups of oil, then add the garlic cloves and fry until golden.
- Add the whole red chillies, the rest of the oil and all the spices. Simmer on very low heat for 45min-1 hour.
- Blend with a hand blender and strain.
- With the oil at room temperature, add the octopus, cover with foil and cook in the oven for 3-4 hours at 130-150 °C.

Tamarind chutney

2 blocks seedless tamarind
3.2 litres water
5 cups sugar
55 g cumin powder
55 g chilli powder
30 g ginger powder

- Mix all ingredients and simmer for one hour.
- Spin with a hand blender and strain.

Tamarind octopus pudding

225 g octopus gel (when the oil cools after cooking the octopus, a purple gel forms at the bottom. Strain the oil to extract the gel)
550 g tamarind chutney
2-5 g Ultratex-3 food starch
2 tbsp ginger juice
2 tbsp lime juice
2 tbsp tamarind chutney masala
salt to taste

- In a bowl, over ice, add all the ingredients except the Ultratex-3.
- Add the Ultratex-3 while blending with a hand blender until it reaches a pudding-like consistency.

To serve

Thinly slice the octopus, baby heirloom tomatoes, Persian cucumbers, and red onion. Arrange on a plate and add dots of the tamarind octopus pudding. Sprinkle with chaat masala, sev, olive oil, sea salt and micro coriander. Serve cold.

Red Snapper and Moley Foam

Serves 2-3

Ingredients

Red snapper

1-2 small red snappers
2 silicon baking mats

- Fillet, debone and skin the fish. Reserve the fillets.
- Scrape off any extra meat and blood off the skin, brush with oil and place between two silicon mats.
- Put a weight on top of the skin and cook in the oven at 180°C until crisp.

Moley foam

1 onion, small dices
2 tbsp ginger, diced
1 tsp turmeric
1.5 litres coconut milk

- Brown the onions and ginger, add the turmeric and coconut milk. Simmer till it thickens.
- Spin in the blender and pass through a chinois.
- Add 1 kg of the mixture to the ISI gun. Use 2-3 NO2 charges to create a foam that holds on the plate.

Tadka

½ cup canola oil
4 tbsp black mustard seeds
½ tsp asafoetida
15 curry leaves
2-3 whole dried red chillies

- Heat the oil and add the asafoetida. Add the mustard seeds and let them crackle.
- Add the red chillies and the curry leaves.
- Keep on low heat until the leaves turn crispy.

To serve

Sear the snapper and baste it in butter. Shoot the foam out of the ISI gun, then place the snapper on top. Spoon the tadka over the fish and garnish with the skin chips.

Kerala Crab Curry

Serves 2

Ingredients

Kerala sauce

1 small onion, diced
8 curry leaves
(4 for the sauce base and 4 for the tadka)
950 ml coconut milk
1-2 pc smoked kokum
1 tbsp mustard seeds
salt to taste

- Fry the onions and 4 curry leaves in oil.
- Add the coconut milk and kokum to this and simmer for 10-15 min, then purée the sauce.
- Fry the mustard seeds and remaining curry leaves in oil and add this to the sauce.

Soft shell crab

1-2 soft shell crabs
128 g chickpea flour
32 g cornstarch
1tsp red chilli flakes
1 tbsp salt
water for consistency

- Clean the crabs thoroughly.
- Mix all the other ingredients to make a thick batter.
- Dip the crabs in the batter, then deep fry.

To serve

Pour the sauce in a bowl and place the crab on top.
Garnish with pieces of fresh baby coconut flesh.

Saffron Panna Cotta

Serves 6-8

Ingredients

Panna cotta

950 g heavy cream
64 g sugar
½ tsp ground cardamom
1 pinch of saffron
5 gelatine sheets

- Heat the heavy cream and sugar and steep the cardamom and saffron.
- Bloom the gelatine and temper into the cream.
- Pour the mixture into moulds and chill.

Yogurt lime sorbet

3.5 kg low-fat yogurt
1 kg sugar
11 tbsp lime juice
1 ½ tsp lime zest

- Melt the sugar with the lime juice and lime zest.
- Mix with the yogurt, place in an ice cream machine and spin and freeze.

Watermelon Shorba

Serves 2

Ingredients

Watermelon soup

1 seedless watermelon
1-2 kaffir lime leaves
15 g sliced ginger
½ a stalk of lemon grass

Green chilli basil seeds

2 tbsp basil seeds
1 green chillie
475 ml warm water
salt to taste

- Cut off the rind of watermelon and cut into large dice.
- Tear the kaffir lime leaves and add to the watermelon with the ginger and lemon grass.
- Roughly mash the watermelon and let it marinate for two hours.
- Spin in a blender and hang in a cheese cloth overnight.
- Add half the water and the green chilli into a blender and spin until combined. Strain.
- Add this to the basil seeds. Keep stirring and adding water until the mix is thoroughly hydrated.

Coriander oil

5 coriander bunches
475 ml canola oil

- Remove the stems from the coriander and blanch and shock the leaves in ice water. Squeeze out as much moisture as possible.
- Roughly chop up the coriander and spin in the blender with enough oil to make a paste (the less oil you put the stronger the final product will be).
- Allow the mixture to chill in a bowl over ice, then spin it in the blender again. Hang it in a cheese cloth overnight.
- The final product should be very dark, almost black, but bright green when put onto a plate.

To serve

Garnish the bowl with basil seeds and a bit of micro shiso. Pour the soup into a sauce pourer, add about 1 tbsp of coriander oil to the top and serve.

YOU DESERVE TO WAKE UP HAPPY
jcpenney

Lahsooni Gobi

Serves 4

Ingredients

Batter

115 g all purpose flour
115 g rice flour
50 g cornstarch
1 tbsp chilli flakes
2 tsp salt
30 ml oil
water
1-2 cauliflowers

- In a large bowl, mix together cornstarch, chilli flakes, and salt.
- Add oil and then water, stirring until consistency is thick but able to drip off your finger.
- Coat florets in batter and fry until lightly golden. Remove to a rack and let cool.

Tomato garlic chutney

225 g ketchup
55 g tomato purée
1 tbsp paprika
1 tbsp chilli powder
55 g chopped garlic
1 tbsp ketchup
salt to taste

- Sweat the garlic but do not brown.
- Add the rest of the ingredients and let simmer for 15 minutes.

To serve

Plate the sauce. Place the cauliflower on to it and garnish with micro coriander.

Tandoori Quail

Serves 6–8

Ingredients

Quail marination

450 g red currants
3 tbsp fennel seeds
3 tbsp cloves
6 tsp pomegranate juice
1 tbsp garam masala
2 tbsp deghi mirch
3 tsp palm sugar
1.5 kg hung yogurt
5 ½ tbsp ginger garlic paste
3–5 quails

- Toast the fennel and the cloves and add the red currants, pomegranate juice, spices and sugar.
- Cook down into a paste, spin in a blender and pass through a chinos cloth.
- After this cools, mix with the hung yogurt and ginger garlic paste.

Swiss chard

1 kg chopped Swiss chard leaves
1 tbsp chopped ginger and garlic
1 pinch cumin seeds
1 pinch chopped mint

- Toast the cumin and sauté the ginger and garlic
- To this mix, add the Swiss chard. Garnish with mint.

Yellow daal

500 g bengal gram, washed thrice
500 g red lentils, washed thrice
500 g green gram, washed thrice
700 ml water
1 tbsp turmeric powder
1 cup whole green chillies
1 tbsp chopped garlic
1 tsp asafoetida
1 tsp cumin seeds
½ cup chopped tomato
½ cup chopped coriander
2 tbsp oil

- In a large pot, mix together all the lentils, water, salt, turmeric powder and green chillies.
- Bring to a boil and let it simmer till the daal breaks apart.
- Heat oil in a pan and add cumin and asafoetida. In this, brown the garlic and add the tomatoes.
- Add this to the daal and garnish with coriander.

To serve

Cook the quail in the tandoor. First plate the lentils, then the Swiss chard and then the quail on top. Garnish with coriander oil and micro shiso.

Bagara Baingan

Serves 2

Ingredients

Eggplant sauce

3-4 tbsp oil
10 g dried whole red chillies
2 tsp whole coriander
2 tsp whole cumin
1 ½ tsp black mustard seeds
½ tsp curry leaves
65 g ginger, finely chopped
65 g garlic, finely chopped
40 g peanuts, unsalted and not roasted
4-5 white onions, chopped
8 tbsp white sesame seeds
70 g shredded, dried, unsweetened coconut
¼ block tamarind
1 litre water
salt to taste

- Heat the oil in a large pot and fry the whole spices until fragrant.
- Add garlic and ginger and cook for another 5-7 minutes.
- Add nuts and cook until they start to soften, then add onions and cook until lightly browned.
- Add sesame seeds and coconut and cook for another 5 minutes.
- In a bowl, dissolve tamarind in hot water to create about two litres of tamarind water.
- Add tamarind water, salt, and remaining water to pot and cook for another 10 to 15 minutes
- Purée with a stick blender and transfer in batches to a food processor to create a thin, smooth curry.

Baingan

2-3 tbsp oil
3-4 curry leaves
2 dried red chillies
1 ½ tsp mustard seeds
355 ml eggplant sauce
2 tsp tamarind chutney
5 pieces eggplant, cross-hatched at the bottom and deep-fried until cooked through

To serve

Heat oil in a pan over medium-high heat and add curry leaves, chillies, and mustard seeds. When mustard seeds start to pop, add eggplant sauce and tamarind chutney and bring up to a simmer. Add eggplant and cover until heated through.

e are what
repeatedly do.
cellence, therefore,
not an act, but
habit. —Aristotle
@dorseyskitchen

GOVERNOR
U S SENATOR

Masaledaar Lamb Chops

Serves 3

Ingredients

Marination

500 g yogurt (hung in cheese cloth overnight)
500 g sour cream
940 g heavy cream
7 tbsp ginger paste
3½ tbsp garlic paste
8 tbsp cashew paste
60 ml oil
1 tbsp meat tenderiser
6 tsp deghi mirch
60 ml malt vinegar
3 tbsp lemon juice
6 tsp garam masala

Pomegranate sauce reduction

1.5 litre pomegranate juice
2 bay leaves
1½ tsp cumin
1 tsp green cardamom
1 ½ tsp coriander seeds
½ tsp cloves
¼ tsp whole white pepper
½ tsp whole black pepper
900 g brown butter (adjust amount for desired consistency)
3-4 tbsp xanthan gum
salt to taste

- Mix spices with pomegranate juice and simmer for 15 min.
- Spin the mixture in the blender and pass through a cheese cloth.
- Add the xanthan gum to the pomegranate reduction.
- Melt the brown butter (it cannot be too hot or the sauce will break) and add while whisking. Add salt to taste.

Potatoes

6-10 potatoes peeled and cut in shapes
2.2 kg lamb fat
2.8 litre canola oil
225 g deghi mirch
225 g garam masala
120 g salt

- Grind the lamb fat, mix everything together and simmer for three hours, then strain.
- Cover potatoes in oil and cook in the oven at 375°C for 20-30 min depending on the size.
- When they are cooked through, cool them off and pan-sear the potatoes.

To serve

Plate the sauce and add the potatoes. Place the lamb chops on top and garnish with micro coriander

Saag Paneer

Serves 4

Ingredients

Spinach purée

225 g baby spinach
1 tomato, diced
1 onion, diced
3 green chillies, chopped
1tbsp chopped ginger
1tbsp choppedgarlic
1tbsp tomato purée
475 g cream
spice blend: turmeric, methi leaves, red chilli powder, ground cumin, ground coriander (1 tsp of each)

- Brown onions, ginger and garlic and add chopped tomatoes and green chillies. Cook for two minutes.
- Add tomato purée and spices and cook for 1-2 minutes. Add the cream and reduce it till it thickens slightly.
- Turn the heat to full blast, add the spinach and sauté for about 20-30 seconds.
- Spread out the mixture on a sheet tray and put it into the freezer quickly to preserve the colour.
- Once cool, spin in the blender until smooth. Salt to taste

Paneer mix

3 egg yolks
700 g crumbled paneer
50 g all purpose flour
10 g salt

- Pulse all ingredients in the food processor until combined (add a little warm water if needed).
- Bring a pot of salted water with a little olive oil to a simmer and turn the heat on low.
- Quenelle the mixture into the poaching water to form gnocchi. Flip the gnocchi after 15 minutes and after 10 minutes more of cooking remove from heat and chill.

To serve

Steam the gnocchi and glaze with butter. Heat the spinach purée, sauté some baby spinach mix in a bit of the purée and plate it with the gnocchi on top. Garnish with an Omani lemon and a deghi mirch spiced chip

Falooda

Serves 4

Ingredients

Rose semifreddo

500 g heavy cream whipped into soft peaks
7 egg yolks
3 eggs
½ tsp salt
266 g sugar
110 g glucose
315 g rose syrup
4 sheets gelatine

- Whip the cream and set aside.
- Whip together the eggs and salt and bring the sugar up to 120°C. Bloom the gelatine.
- Add everything (except the cream) to the egg mixture, cool to room temperature and fold into the whipped cream.
- Place in moulds and freeze.

Lime granita

700 ml water
zest of 2 limes
225 g sugar
180 g lime juice
120 g coriander
1 tsp salt
4 tbsp gin

- Bring the water, lime zest and sugar to a boil and strain.
- Purée the coriander, lime juice and salt.
- Mix together everything and freeze.

Crème anglaise

1 litre milk
1 litre heavy cream
200 g sugar
3 vanilla beans
16 egg yolks
200 g sugar

- Bring the milk, cream, sugar and vanilla beans to a boil.
- Whisk together the egg yolks and temper into the milk cream mixture.
- Cook slowly until mixture is thick enough to coat the back of a spoon.

To serve

Place the semifreddo in a bowl with the granita and pour the crème anglaise by the side.

Frances Atkins

A Fellow of The Master Chefs of Great Britain and a holder of a Michelin Star, Frances Atkins has cooked all her life with passion and enthusiasm. Her food is free spirited and is backed by classical technique. The Michelin recognitions have made her one of the very few female chefs with an international reputation.

She appears regularly on national television and radio channels. Frances is currently busy filming a series of programmes and films, due to be launched in 2013/2014. Her culinary reputation and total dedication precede her.

Menu 1

Three Smoked Fish, Pickled Cucumber, Pistachio Crisp

Truffled Golden Quail, Lychee, Jasmine Mist

Peach Praliné, Coconut Sorbet, Rose Petal Jelly

Menu 2

Vegetable Tartare, Pea Brûlée

Slow-cooked Shoulder of Lamb, Warm Sheep Milk Panna Cotta, Moorland Flavours

Chocolate Truffle, Marinated Strawberries, Tonka Bean Ice Cream

Menu 3

Basil and Tomato Sorbet, Gazpacho, Langoustine, Samphire

Saddle of Red Deer, Black Currant, Sour Cream, Liquorice, Puy Lentils

Verbena Panna Cotta, Rose Petal Jelly, Pistachio Vacherin

Menu 4

Rhubarb, Watermelon Jelly, Granola, Savoury Madeleine

Spiced Freekeh, Roasted Vegetables, Smoked Avocado

Caramel, Black Currant, Liquorice Chilled Mousse, Poppy Seed Feuillentine,
Chilli and Mango

Menu 5

Yorkshire Potted Beef, Pickled Vegetables

Roast Turbot, Sea Scallop, Lovage, Preserved Lemon

Chocolate and Marshmallow Truffle

Three Smoked Fish, Pickled Cucumber, Pistachio Crisp

Serves 12

Ingredients

Taramasalata

500 g cod roe soaked in water
160 g fresh white breadcrumbs
2 lemons, juiced
200 g crème fraîche
6 g sea salt

- Remove the skin from the cod roe.
- Combine all ingredients together in a blender and pulse until mixed but not puréed.

Salt-cured cod

500 g cod belly
60 g sea salt
35 g sugar
1 lemon, zest
3 sprigs each of parsley and dill

- Mix the salt, sugar, dill, parsley and lemon zest in a bowl.
- Coat the cod and wrap in cling film tightly.
- Cure for 3 days, turning each day.

Smoked cod brandade

salt-cured cod
150 g mash potato
150 g olive oil
2 cloves of garlic, finely diced
2 banana shallots, finely diced
5 g of ground cardamom
15 g chopped fresh parsley

- Rinse the cod under cold water and pat dry. Set up a smoker and hot smoke the cod for about 5 minutes on the heat, then remove from the heat and leave to rest for 2 minutes.
- Weigh 300 g of the cod, set the remaining aside for garnish.
- Cook the shallots and garlic gently in the olive oil until tender.
- Flake the cod into the mash, combine with the remaining ingredients and fold together.

Pistachio loaf

375 g strong organic white flour
6 g salt
18.5 g honey
18.5 g olive oil
10 g fresh yeast
210 g water
50 g peeled green pistachios

- Mix the flour, salt and pistachios together.
- Mix the yeast with water in body temperature and then add the honey and olive oil.
- Place the dry mixture in a stand mixer fitted with a dough hook.
- Add the wet ingredients and mix on low speed until coming away from the edges.
- Cover with cling film and let proof for 2 hours.
- Knead well, shape into a lined and greased loaf tin, let it rise again then bake at 160°C for 20-25 minutes.
- Leave to cool on a wire rack.

Pistachio croutons

Pistachio loaf
Olive oil

- Set oven to 130°C.
- Slice the pistachio bread thinly, about 2 mm thick, and tear into random size pieces.
- Place on a baking tray and sprinkle olive oil, bake for around 15 minutes or until very crispy.

Smoked mackerel rolled in pickled cucumber

300 g white wine vinegar
200 g caster sugar
1 sprig of thyme
1 cucumber, peeled
1 fillet of smoked mackerel

- Combine the vinegar, sugar and thyme in a pan, bring to a boil and simmer for 5 minutes, leave in the fridge to cool.
- Using a speed peeler to peel ribbon style lengths of the cucumber, trim to 10 cm x 3 cm pieces and set aside.
- Remove skin from the mackerel and cut either side of the centre pin bones of the mackerel to remove any bones, then flake into bite sized pieces.
- Drag the cucumber through the vinegar and place a piece of mackerel at one end, roll tightly.

Peas

300 g fresh peas in the pod
water and salt for cooking

- Place water and salt in a pan and bring to a boil.
- Remove the peas from the pods.
- Quickly blanch the peas for about 30 seconds and then refresh.
- Remove peas from the shells.
- Mix with about 1 teaspoon of the white wine pickle mixture.

To garnish

goat milk yogurt
lemon sorrel
red veined sorrel
watercress
fried free range egg

Truffled Golden Quail, Lychee, Jasmine Mist

Serves 10

Ingredients

2 tins of lychee (567 g)
liquid from 1 tin only
5 quails
10 large leaves of spinach (blanched and refreshed)
6 cardamom pods (crushed and chopped)
50 g shallot (diced finely)
80 g ground almond
20 g ground pistachio
½ lemon zest
3 g lemon thyme
50 g softened butter
40 g fresh white bread crumbs
1 medium-size truffle
1 sheet of gold leaf

Pea Purée

400 g peas
150 g cream (reduced by half)

- Cook the peas until very soft. Refresh. Blitz together and correct the seasoning.

Almond Snow

200 g toasted flaked almonds
800 g semi skimmed milk
4 g salt
24 g sugar

- Mix and simmer for 30 minutes and infuse for 1 hour. Strain and season with salt and sugar. Freeze in Pac container. Pacotize and tray in freezer.

- Mix all the ingredients, season with salt and pepper, almond oil and truffle.
- Place spinach leaf on cling film and place a small amount of mixture onto the spinach.
- Roll into a boudin size.
- Remove the breast of the quail, keeping the wing bone on.
- Peel back the skin and place 2 slices of truffle on each breast.
- Remove the cling film from around the boudin.
- Place onto quail breast and then replace the skin on top.
- Wrap in cling film.
- Vac-pack and sous vide for 45 minutes at 64°C (low heat).
- Remove sous vide pack and brush with butter. Pan-fry until golden brown.
- Slice lengthways and decorate with gold leaf.
- Serve on pea purée, almond snow and celery leaf, pea sprouts.

To serve (per portion)

1 celery leaf
peas (cooked and salted)
1 pea sprout
1 tsp almond snow
1 jasmine mist tea bag

Serve on pea purée, peas and pea sprouts, celery leaf and almond snow in mini thermic glasses with jasmine tea.

Peach Praliné, Coconut Sorbet, Rose Petal Jelly

Serves 6

Ingredients

Praliné tuile

100 g sugar
100 g fondant
100 g glucose
75 g flaked almonds

- Add sugar, fondant and glucose into a pan and heat until it forms a light caramel.
- Warm flaked almonds.
- Add to the light caramel and pour onto oiled surface, roll out and leave to cool.
- When cooled, blitz until a rough powder is formed.
- Sprinkle onto warmed greaseproof tray and bake at 180°C for 8-10 minutes.
- Remove from oven and cut to size.

Rose petal jelly

30 ml rosewater
35 g sugar
35 g water
100 g poaching liquor from the peach
2 leaves of gelatine

- Warm the water, sugar, rosewater and poaching liquor.
- Soften the gelatine leaves and dissolve in the liquor.
- Pour into a mould and leave to set.

Cardamom crumb

50 g sugar
65 g ground almonds
35 g grain flour
a pinch of salt
32 g melted butter
6 cardamom pods (crushed and deseeded)

- Mix all the ingredients together.
- Bake at 150°C for 15-20 minutes.
- When cool break up into crumbs.

Peach roché

250 g poached peaches
65 g poaching liquor
3½ gelatine leaves

- Soften gelatine leaves.
- Add to the warmed liquor.
- Blitz all together until smooth.
- Pass through a sieve.

Coconut sorbet

500 g coconut, milk and pulp mixed together
100 g sugar
150 g water

Dissolve the sugar in and water then add the coconut and churn.

To serve

On the plate, sandwich together the praliné tuile, the peach roche and the coconut sorbet. Place small piles of cardamom crumb around the plate and place the sorbet, rose petal jelly and peach roche on top.

Vegetable Tartare, Pea Brûlée

Serves 8

Ingredients

120 g frozen peas blanched and refreshed
280 g cream (whipped)
4 egg yolks
a pinch of salt
15 g sugar

- Blanch the peas and refresh.
- Bring cream to a boil, add the peas and blitz. Push through a sieve.
- Whisk yolks, sugar and salt. Pour peas into mixture.
- Place in dish 20 cm x 15 cm x 5 cm depth.
- Put dish in bain-marie and cover with film.
- Cook for 15 minutes at 150°C (low heat).
- Cool and chill.
- Cut out to size.
- Sprinkle sugar on top and blow-torch the sugar to caramelise.

Vegetable tartare

1 small carrot
50 g butternut squash
1 stick of celery
50 g celeriac
50 g cucumber peeled, deseeded and dried
4 semi-dried tomatoes
2 g capers
1 tbsp chives

Vinaigrette

60 ml oil
20 ml vinegar
10 g honey
1 tbsp wholegrain mustard
salt and pepper to taste

- Blend all ingredients except oil. Feed oil slowly into mix so that it is thick.
- Dice the vegetables, ¼ cm.
- Mix together with tomato, chives, capers and bind with vinaigrette.
- Pack in oblong moulds and garnish with seasonal vegetables, leaf and pea brûlée.
- Add extra vinaigrette for garnish.

Slow-cooked Shoulder of Lamb, Warm Sheep Milk Panna Cotta, Moorland Flavours

Serves 6

Ingredients

Sheep milk panna cotta

225 g sheep milk yogurt
2 free range eggs
salt

- Beat yogurt and eggs together.
- Butter 4 egg cups.
- Pour into egg cups and cover with foil.
- Cook in bain marie, at 150°C (low heat) for 20 minutes.

Dry spice rub on lamb

1 green chilli
2 sprigs of rosemary
35 g ginger, peeled
2 g cumin seeds
2 g caraway seeds
2 g fennel seeds
2 g coriander seeds
1 small shoulder of lamb, chopped into four pieces
1 carrot
1 leek
1 onion
1 stick of celery
500 ml stock (water or red wine)
1 tsp almond oil
1 dessert spoon gorse flower

- Finely chop and mix together all the ingredients.
- Trim most of the fat off the lamb and rub in the crushed spices.
- Season with salt and pepper.
- Chop the vegetables.
- Brown them with the lamb and seal in a casserole dish with a lid.
- Add the stock, cover and cook slowly until soft and the meat falls off the bone – approx. 2 hours on moderate heat at 180°C.

Puffed rice

30 g wild rice
50 ml cooking oil

- Heat the oil until smoking. Pull off the heat and carefully place the rice in the oil so it sizzles and puffs.
- Remove from pan and drain on kitchen paper.
- When the lamb is cooked remove from liquor and put through a sieve.
- Reduce the liquor by half and add the almond oil and gorse flower.
- Pour over the lamb and serve with the warm panna cotta and puffed rice.

Chocolate Truffle, Marinated Strawberries, Tonka Bean Ice Cream

Serves 8

Ingredients

3 eggs
57 g sugar
255 g chocolate
44 ml brandy
2 tsp instant coffee
170 g cream (whipped)

- Heat the cream. Add the chocolate, brandy and coffee. Fold into the whisked eggs and sugar
- Pour mixture into a lined tray (12" x 6") and bake for 20 minutes at 150°C.
- Stand for 5 minutes and freeze until chilled.

Chocolate ganash

200 g chocolate
200 g whipped cream, brought to a boil
50 g glucose

- Pour over the chocolate cake and leave to set.

Tonka bean ice cream

6 egg yolks
125 g sugar
250 g whipped cream
250 ml milk
2 tonka beans

- Whisk the yolks and sugar.
- Grate the tonka beans into the milk and cream, bring to a boil. Pour over the yolks and sugar.
- Return to the pan and cook on low heat until slightly thickened.
- Cool and freeze for the ice cream machine. (If not using an ice cream machine keep churning as it is freezing.)

Marinated strawberries

- Slice the strawberries lengthways and marinate in white balsamic vinegar.
- Serve with chocolate truffle and tonka bean ice cream.

Basil and Tomato Sorbet, Gazpacho, Langoustine, Samphire

Serves 8

Ingredients

100 g vine plum tomatoes
100 g heritage tomatoes
25 g semi-dried tomatoes
25 g sweet cherry tomatoes
25 g isomalt
75 g glucose
35 g sugar
25 g basil leaf
4 g salt
75 g water

- Boil water, salt and sugars. Add basil leaf and infuse for 10 minutes. Strain.
- Pour liquid over tomatoes and blitz.
- Either freeze and put into an ice cream machine or churn in ice cream machine.

Gazpacho

1 cucumber, peeled
200 g ripe tomatoes
1 green pepper
1 roasted red pepper
2 cloves of garlic
½ of a red onion
15 g basil
2 ml extra virgin olive oil
7 g sea salt
20 g white balsamic

- Chop ingredients and leave to steep for 1 hour.
- Blitz and pass through strainer.
- Check consistency and put a handful of ice into mixture and chill.

Pickled samphire

20 g samphire
5 g white vinegar
5 g sugar

- Bring vinegar to boil. Add sugar and samphire.
- Sauté 2 langoustine in oil, butter and garlic and serve with each portion.

Saddle of Red Deer, Black Currant, Sour Cream, Liquorice, Puy Lentils

Serves 4

Ingredients

1 saddle of venison
100 g black currants
8 baby beetroots
1 carrot, finely chopped
1 shallot, finely chopped
1 stick of celery, finely chopped
1 tsp sugar
100 ml water
250 g puy lentils
25 g girolle mushrooms
salt and pepper (a pinch each)
5 g chilli powder
½ tsp liquorice essence
20 g butter

- Seal the saddle of venison on all sides and place in a buttered dish with black currants, sugar, water and beetroot.
- Place in the oven at 200°C (moderate heat) for 20 minutes.
- Remove the meat and beetroot from the dish and leave to rest.
- Pass the rest of the liquid through a sieve and check the seasoning.
- Wash and cook the lentils separately until soft. Drain well and add the finely chopped carrot, shallot and celery with the butter. Reheat.
- Slice the venison, place the black currants on the plate with the venison on top. Spoon the lentils and mushrooms around it.

Saffron pancakes with sour cream

10 g sour cream
200 g self raising flour
1 tsp baking powder
10 ml milk
1 egg
2 saffron threads

- Mix the flour, baking powder, egg, milk and saffron to a batter.
- Spoon on to a griddle in small amounts and cook each side.
- Fill with sour cream and present on the plate with the venison.

Verbena Panna Cotta, Rose Petal Jelly, Pistachio Vacherin

Serves 8

Ingredients

Panna cotta

(25 ml per person, makes 8)

120 g milk
10 g lemon verbena
30 g spinach
10 g sugar
70 g cream
1½ gelatine leaves

- Soften gelatine in cold water.
- Bring milk, sugar and verbena to a boil. Remove from the heat and allow the ingredients to infuse.
- Heat the cream and add softened gelatine. Then add spinach and verbena milk.
- Blitz and pass.
- Pour into moulds to set in the fridge.

Rose petal jelly

45 g raspberries
45 g strawberries
90 g caster sugar
200 g rose wine
13 g rose water
3 gelatine leaves

- Bring the sugar, rose, strawberries, and raspberries to a boil and simmer for 5 minutes. Pass through a sieve.
- Soften the gelatine. Add to the strained liquid with the rose water and mix thoroughly.
- Place in tray to set in the fridge.

Pistachio vacherin

40 g pistachio paste
150 g white chocolate
100 g cream
50 g egg white
100 g sugar

Meringue

- Whisk the egg white until semi-stiff. Whisk in the caster sugar.
- Pipe 10 cm long, 1 cm wide sticks on a tray covered with silicone paper. Leave to dry in warming cupboard or cook off at 100°C (very, very low heat).

Pistachio cream

- Boil the cream and the pistachio paste together.
- Stir in the white chocolate. Cool and refrigerate.

To serve

Empty out the panna cotta. Dice the rose petal jelly. Sandwich the meringue together with pistachio cream. Garnish with sugared pistachio and dried rose petals.

Rhubarb, Watermelon Jelly, Granola, Savoury Madeleine

60 Portions (Amuse-bouche Size)

Ingredients

Granola

1 cup rolled oats
¼ cup almonds, sliced
2 tbsp light brown sugar
2 tbsp maple syrup
1½ tbsp olive oil
¼ tsp salt
½ tsp mace

- Line a baking sheet with parchment paper.
- Mix oats and almonds.
- Bring the sugar and maple syrup, oil and salt to a boil.
- Pour over the oat mixture and toss to combine.
- Spread oats onto the baking sheet and bake for 10 minutes until golden and dry.
- Store in an air-tight container.

Rhubarb, watermelon jelly

220 g raw rhubarb
50 g sugar
(vac-pack and cook in steamer for 15 minutes at low heat)
50 g white wine
200 g cooked baby golden beetroot
3 limes, zested and juiced
375 ml watermelon water
160 g sugar
15 g mixed garden flowers (picked)

- Cook the rhubarb and refresh, keeping the liquid.
- Slice the beetroot and layer on a cling filmed (40 cm x 27 cm) tray.
- Pat dry the rhubarb and dice into 1 cm squares.
- Arrange on top of the beetroot.
- Add the lime zest and garden flowers and chill.

Jelly

750 g watermelon juice
25 g lime juice
100 g rhubarb
150 g sugar
2.5 g gellan gum – type F
2.5 g gellan gum – type LT100

- Mix all together.
- Warm 200 g of the liquid.
- Mix 10 g of sugar with 5 g of gellan gum, whisking all the time.
- Bring to a boil.
- Add the rest of the liquid, whisking well.
- Pour slowly over a tray and chill.

Savoury madeleine

90 g butter
15 g honey
90 g flour
1 tsp baking powder
2 free range eggs
15 g sugar
1 tsp curry powder
6 cardamom pods
½ tsp fennel seeds
½ tsp chopped thyme

- Melt butter and honey. Cool and mix with the rest of the ingredients.
- Butter and flour a 'mini' madeleine tin.
- Pipe in the mixture.
- Cook at 200°C (moderate heat) for 8 minutes, until golden brown.

To assemble the jelly

Cut the jelly into squares. Put a quenelle of crème fraîche on top. Add the granola, flowers and savoury madeleine. You can also add caviar after the quenelled crème fraîche on top. Follow this with flowers and savoury madeleine.

Spiced Freekeh, Roasted Vegetables, Smoked Avocado

Serves 4

Ingredients

1 carrot
1 small butternut squash
1 small parsnip
1 red pepper
1 chilli
1 courgette flower
1 aubergine
girolle mushroom
1 tsp cardamom
1 tsp cumin
½ tsp nutmeg
1 tsp chilli powder
fresh herbs
200 g freekeh
100 g dried black olive powder
(dry black olives in a warm place overnight and grind into a powder)
1 avocado
(smoke lightly, purée and season well)
30 g pistachio nuts (peeled)

- Finely chop all the vegetables and roast lightly in oil with cardamom, cumin, nutmeg and chilli.
- Cook the freekeh in salted water until soft.
- Drain well and chop fresh herbs on it.
- Season with salt and pepper and a dash of butter.

Tomato and vanilla sauce

4 tomatoes
1 vanilla pod
1 tbsp white wine vinegar
1 small shallot
50 g sugar

- Chop shallot and tomato and put in a pan with white wine vinegar, sugar and water, adding salt and pepper.
- Cover and cook on low heat slowly until puréed.
- Blitz in food blender and pass through a sieve.

To serve

Place all the components together on a plate and finish with pistachio nuts.

Caramel, Black Currant, Liquorice Chilled Mousse, Poppy Seed Feuillentine, Chilli and Mango

Serves 8

Ingredients

Black currant caramel chilled mousse

15 g liquorice stick
50 g sugar
100 g water
200 g black currants
180 g semi-whipped cream
2½ gelatine leaves, softened

- Bring the liquorice, sugar, water and black currants to a boil. Simmer for 15 minutes. Leave to stand for one hour. Pass through a sieve. (The weight should now be 240 g of black currant purée.)
- Gently heat 40 g of the black currant purée and mix in the soaked gelatine.
- Add to the remaining 200 g semi-whipped cream. Fold in the black currant purée and gelatine.
- Pour into a lined mould (1 cm deep) and place in the fridge to semi set.

Caramel

60 g sugar
(heat mildly to make caramel)
80 g cream
100 g egg custard
2½ gelatine leaves, soaked
180 g semi whipped cream
a pinch of chilli powder

- Warm the custard and mix in the soaked gelatine. Stir into the caramel sauce. Cool to body temperature.
- Fold in the semi-whipped cream.
- Pour caramel mousse on top of the semi-set black currant mousse, 1 cm deep, and chill.
- Once set, freeze.

Mango sorbet

1 kg mango purée
200 g sugar
300 ml water
20 ml brandy

- Bring the sugar and water to a boil. Stir in the brandy and purée, then churn and freeze.
- Once frozen, use a 2.5 cm parisienne to scoop 2 balls per plate on a large flat tray and freeze.

Poppy seed feuillantine

50 g puff pastry
20 g icing sugar
8 g poppy seed

- Roll out the pastry to 3 mm thickness.
- Cover half with sieved icing sugar.
- Fold in half. Roll until 3 mm thick. Repeat.
- Sprinkle the poppy seeds on the top and cook for 15 minutes at 170°C (moderate heat) in between 2 sheets of greaseproof paper with another tray weighing it down.
- Remove from the oven.
- Cool and cut into fingers (3 cm x 12 cm).

Chilli garnish

85 g whole chillies
85 g sugar
85 ml water

- Deseed the chilli. Cook in sugar and water until soft.
- Cut into fine strips and dry.

Chilled mousse garnish

25 ml mango coulis (5 mangoes)
liquorice coulis (1 swipe per plate)
gold leaf
50 ml cream/egg custard (per plate)
frozen black currants – 4 per plate.
sweetened mascarpone (2 dots per plate)
5 strips of chillies
2 balls of sorbet

Sweetened mascarpone

2 kg mascarpone
6 leaves of gelatine
icing sugar to taste
2 vanilla pods, seeded

- Soften gelatine. Warm 200 g mascarpone. Whisk in gelatine and vanilla.
- Beat into the remaining mascarpone with the icing sugar. Put into piping bags.

To serve

Place a slice of the mousse on the plate with lines of liquorice and mango coulis. 2 Parisienne scoops of sorbet — one to the top right and one to the bottom left of the mousse. Place the gold leaf on top of the sorbet. Lay sliced mango on top of the mousse and finish with feuillatine biscuit. Place the frozen black currants around the mousse with the chilli and a little egg custard.

Yorkshire Potted Beef, Pickled Vegetables

Serves 6

INGREDIENTS

1 kg trimmed raw sirloin
1 onion
100 ml port
2 litres veal stock
100 g butter

- Dice the beef into small cubes and chop the onion.
- Brown together in a pan with 50 g of butter.
- Add the port and veal stock.
- Simmer on low heat for an hour until the beef is tender and the liquor has reduced into the meat.
- Butter a mould and press down the contents in it firmly. You may add other ingredients of your choice such as foie gras, pressed ham or marinated raisins.
- Seal with melted butter and chill.

Roast Turbot, Sea Scallop, Lovage, Preserved Lemon

Serves 4

Ingredients

1 turbot (approx. 2 kg)
4 sea scallops
1 lemon (whole – boiled in water until soft)
1 bunch lovage
1 tsp ground cardamom
1 head of celery
caraway tuile
50 g butter
200 ml white wine

Caraway tuile

125 g mashed potato
38 g egg white
10 g olive oil
8 g caraway seeds

- Mix the potato with the egg white and pass through a drum sieve.
- Spread thinly on silicone paper, on 2 trays (30 cm x 15 cm). Sprinkle with the caraway seeds. Bake in the oven for 15-20 minutes until dry at 130°C. Cool and then seal in a deep fat fryer.
- Butter an earthenware dish. Wash and season the turbot. Place with the bunch of lovage, celery and the boiled lemon, sliced thinly. Add salt, pepper and a tsp of ground cardamom and 200 g of white wine or water.
- Place in the oven at 175°C for 25 minutes. Add the Scallops for the final 5 minutes of cooking time.
- Remove from the oven and take the fish off the bone. Place on a plate with the celery and sliced lemon.
- Drain off the juices.
- Thicken the juices with a little butter and serve around the fish with green beans and deep-fried lovage.

Chocolate and Marshmallow Truffle

Serves 6 (Petit-four Size)

Ingredients

Brownie mixture

75 g sugar
1 egg
54 g butter
67 g chocolate
18 g cocoa
18 g flour
25 g white chocolate buttons
25 g hazelnuts, peeled

- Whisk the sugar and the egg together. Add melted butter and chocolate.
- Fold into the rest of the ingredients. Place on a lined silicone tray and cook for 15 minutes at 180°C (moderate heat). Once cooled flatten the top to make an even surface to add the marshmallow.

Marshmallow

250 g sugar
175 g water
32 g glucose syrup
16 g gelatine
35 g egg white

- Mix sugar and water and cook at 121°C (low heat). Add 16 g gelatine. Let it cool.
- Whisk 35 g egg white to a soft peak and slowly pour in the sugar/gelatine solution. Whisk for 4 minutes at a high speed.
- Spread over the chocolate brownie. Leave to set.
- Sieve icing sugar over the top and cut into squares.

Laurie Gear

Born in Dorset in 1967, Laurie Gear was working in restaurants in the seaside town of Lyme Regis during his early teens. He continued this while completing his formal chef training at Weymouth Technical College. Gear met his wife while working in the kitchen of the Combe House hotel in Gittisham and in 2002 they achieved their dream of running their own restaurant, which they named The Artichoke. He did not give up when a fire nearly gutted the premises in Amersham in 2008, instead spending the interim period before its reopening at Noma in Copenhagen, which has been ranked as the best restaurant in the world. When The Artichoke resumed services, it won The Good Food Guide's 2011 Best New Entry award and Gear was awarded a Michelin Rising Star prize.

Menu 1

Fennel Soup with Dorset Crab, Goat Curd Gnocchi and Cucumber Tagliatelle

Pickled Artichokes, Girolle Mushrooms, Hazelnut Emulsion and Hazelnut Vinaigrette

Slow-poached Fillet of Brill, White Onion Mousse, Sea Vegetables, Orange,
Vanilla and Cardamom Reduction

Stokenchurch Duck Breast with Duck Leg Boudin, Pomme Maxime,
Duck Liver Parfait, Pea Purée and Duck Sherry Sauce

Goat Milk Mousse and Sorrel Sorbet

Menu 2

Jerusalem Artichoke Soup

Ravioli of Guinea Fowl with Wild Mushrooms and Sage Beurre Noisette

Fillet of John Dory, Crab and Scallop Boudin, Tomato Terrine and Avocado Cream

Mango and Coconut Mousse, Lime Sherbet and Lime Gel

Menu 3

Honey, Saffron and Pollen Bread

Pan-fried Isle of Skye Scallop, Seaweed Jelly, Pickled Radish and Mouli and Wasabi Foam

Pan-fried Skate Wing, Purple Cauliflower Purée, Pickled Cauliflower and Romanesco,
Caper and Citrus Butter Sauce

Rice Pudding with Toasted Coconut, Mango, Lime Syrup and Gorse Flowers

Preserve

Quince Jelly

Fennel Soup with Dorset Crab and Goat Curd Gnocchi and Cucumber Tagliatelle

Serves 4

Ingredients

Soup

1 fennel bulb
½ clove of garlic
½ onion, medium-sized
1 stick celery
1 banana shallot
500 ml chicken stock
1 medium potato
1 tbsp Pernod

- Finely dice all ingredients and sweat off in a pan.
- Add the Pernod to flame and then add the chicken stock.
- Simmer for 25 minutes and then pass through a chinois.
- Season to taste.

Gnocchi

250 g Desiree or Maris Piper potatoes
50 g pasta flour
25 g semolina flour for dusting
1 tsp Maldon salt
½ free range egg
25 g goat curd (or ricotta)
½ spring onion, finely diced
50 g fresh picked Lyme Bay crab meat
a few sprigs of dill, finely diced

- Bake potatoes in their skins at 200°C until soft and then peel whilst warm.
- Pass through a sieve.
- When cool, gently fold in the other ingredients.
- Season to taste.
- Pipe out the potato mixture into 30 cm lines and cut into even 8 cm x 5 cm pieces.
- Roll in the semolina flour and leave to set in the fridge. This ensures that they keep their shape while cooking.
- Poach in boiling salted water until they float.

To serve

Cucumber, sliced thinly into tagliatelle
olive oil
butter

Gently warm the fennel soup. Fry the gnocchi in a little oil and butter until golden brown. Place a small pile of thinly sliced cucumber tagliatelle into four warmed soup bowls. Place two gnocchi per portion on top and then pour the fennel soup. Garnish with a sprig of dill and a few drops of quality olive oil.

Pickled Artichokes, Girolle Mushrooms, Hazelnut Emulsion and Hazelnut Vinaigrette

Serves 4

Ingredients

Pickled artichokes

500 ml water
50 g white wine vinegar
50 g white wine
¼ tsp coriander seeds
¼ tsp white peppercorns
2 sprigs thyme
¼ bay leaf
8 violet artichokes
¼ teaspoon ascorbic acid
Large bowl of ice cubes
Juice of half a lemon
400 ml water

- Place all measured ingredients in a large pan and bring to a boil. Leave to cool with salt to taste.
- Place ice, water, ascorbic acid and lemon juice in a large bowl.
- Prep the artichokes in iced water.
- Pass the poaching liqueur and poach the artichoke till just cooked. Leave to cool in the cooking liqueur.

Girolle mushroom pickle

100 g girolle mushrooms
20 g Chardonnay vinegar
6 tbsp water
1 g white peppercorns
½ sprig of thyme
1 bay leaf
salt to taste
1 tsp sugar

- Bring all ingredients to a boil.
- Add the girolle mushrooms and turn off the heat.
- Leave to cool in the cooking liquid.

Hazelnut emulsion

2 egg yolks
20 g sherry vinegar
5 g table salt
60 g hazelnut paste
250 g grapeseed oil
250 g hazelnut oil
100 g water

- Place the egg yolks, sherry vincgar, hazelnut paste and salt in a food processor.
- Mix until combined.
- Add the oils slowly to emulsify.
- Finish with a dash of water to form a mayonnaise-like consistency.

Hazelnut vinaigrette

150 g blanched, shelled hazelnuts
1 ¼ bunches micro watercress
150 g Granny Smith apples
2 tbsp groundnut oil
2 tbsp hazelnut oil
1 tbsp white wine vinegar
salt to taste
½ lemon

- Mix groundnut oil with hazelnut oil and white wine vinegar. Add salt and lemon juice.
- Toast the hazelnuts either in a hot pan or a hot oven until golden brown.
- Leave to cool and then roughly chop with a knife.
- Peel and cut the Granny Smith apples in strips and add lemon juice to stop them from browning.
- Dress the plate with the hazelnut emulsion. Arrange the pickled artichokes and girolle mushrooms. Add a smattering of watercress leaves. Add chopped hazelnuts and thin strips of the Granny Smith apples.

Slow-poached Fillet of Brill, White Onion Mousse, Sea Vegetables, Orange, Vanilla and Cardamom Reduction

Serves 4

Ingredients

4 medium or large-sized brill fillets, skinned
150 g samphire
15 g sea beet
20 baby onions split in half and pan-fried in a little butter until the skins lift off

Onion mousse

1 kg white onions
15 g butter
2 bay leaves
50 g Parmesan cheese
150 g apple juice
15 g white wine
100 g double cream

- Peel and thinly slice the onions.
- In a hot pan, sweat onions with the white wine, bay leaves and butter, then add Parmesan.
- Add apple juice and cream and bring to a simmer. Liquidise and pass through a fine sieve.
- The liquid can then be chilled, placed in a cream whipper and put under a gas charge to dispense.

Orange, cardamom and vanilla reduction

3 cardamom pods
1 garlic clove, peeled
⅓ vanilla pod, split
1 tsp caster sugar
10 tbsp fresh orange juice
5 tbsp white wine vinegar

- Mix all ingredients in a pan, bring to a boil and reduce until thick and glossy. Pass through a fine sieve.

Pastry tubes

4 sheets feuille de brick pastry
100 g clarified butter
a handful of black onion seeds

- Brush the sheets of feuille de brick pastry with clarified butter, then wrap around a stainless steel tube lined with greaseproof paper.
- Sprinkle with black onion seeds and bake at 160 °C until golden (approximately 8 minutes). Slide off the tubes while still warm.

To serve

- In a hot pan with a little butter, quickly cook sea vegetables.
- Paint a few brushstrokes of orange sauce onto the plate and place the sea vegetables on top.
- In a little fish stock, gently poach the brill fillets until just cooked (3–4 minutes depending on thickness).
- Pipe the onion mousse into the pastry tubes and place one tube per person on the plate.
- Finish with a row of glazed baby onions.

Stokenchurch Duck Breast with Duck Leg Boudin, Pomme Maxime, Duck Liver Parfait, Pea Purée and Duck Sherry Sauce

Serves 4

Ingredients

4 free range duck breasts

Duck leg boudin

½ chicken breast
1 ¼ egg yolks
4 g brandy
30 g confit and picked duck leg
1 tsp freshly picked marjoram
40 g double cream
a pinch of salt
a pinch of cayenne pepper

- Place the food processor bowl into the freezer until ice cold.
- Place the diced chicken, egg yolks and salt into the cold processor bowl and purée.
- Pass through a drum sieve, then place the purée back into the clean, cold bowl and pour in the cream.
- Add the brandy, cayenne pepper and seasoning and then roll a tester.
- Check the seasoning and texture and adjust with cream and salt.
- Once satisfied with the texture, fold in the picked duck leg and marjoram and roll into a boudin.
- Poach for 10 minutes at 60°C.

Pomme maxime

1 large potato (waxy variety)
clarified butter
a pinch of salt

- Peel and cut the potatoes with a medium round cutter or fondant cutter.
- Slice finely into discs using a mandolin and layer into a semi-circular shape on silicon paper.
- Brush with clarified butter and cover with silicon paper.
- Sandwich between two flat trays and weigh down, then bake in a full-fan oven at 160 °C until golden brown.

Pea purée

1 tbsp chopped shallots
140 g blanched and refreshed peas
50 g milk
50 g double cream
3.5 g butter
salt to taste

- Sweat the sliced shallots in the butter until they have no colour, seasoning as you cook.
- Add half the peas, the double cream and the milk and then bring to a boil.
- Place in the blender to make a purée, then add the rest of the blanched peas.
- Once smooth, season and pass over ice and then leave to chill.

Duck liver parfait

65 g duck livers
13 g foie-gras
30 g double cream
10 g shallots
Half a small clove of garlic
½ egg
6 g brandy
26 g port
26 g Madeira wine
pink salt to season
¼ twist of white pepper

- Place the shallots, garlic, port and Madeira into a pan and reduce until it has a syrupy consistency.
- Place the reduction and all the other ingredients into a blender.
- Pass through a fine sieve.
- Pour into 2 separate medium-sized vacuum-pack bags and poach in a water bath.
- Cook at 64°C for 22 minutes, then check the texture as it may require a little more cooking.
- Put back in cleaned blender and blend until smooth.
- Pass through a sieve and leave to set in the fridge.

Duck sherry sauce

Bones from 1 duck carcass
¼ celery stick
½ carrot
2 garlic cloves
1 white leek
1 sprig of thyme
1 bay leaf
80 ml medium dry sherry
1 juniper berry
1 white peppercorn
400 ml veal stock
400 ml chicken stock
40g duck wings
32 ml sherry vinegar
1 g orange zest
8 g morel trim
2 g rosemary

- Roast off duck carcass, making sure that the bones are clean and offal-free to prevent the sauce from being cloudy.
- In a saucepan, roast off the shallots, carrots, celery and garlic, then add the leek.
- Once they're golden brown, add the aromatics and pour on the sherry vinegar. Reduce until dry.
- Add the sherry and reduce by two-thirds, then pour on the stock. Add the bones and all other ingredients.
- Bring to a simmer, then skim and cook for two hours on low heat.
- Pass through double muslin and reduce to a sauce consistency.

To serve

Pan-fry the duck breast in a hot pan with oil and allow to rest before carving. Brush a sweep of pea purée onto a warm plate. Sprinkle the mushrooms and peas over it. Sit the potato wafer on three pillars of boudin. Spoon a little parfait onto the wafer. Dress the dish with some duck sauce and pea shoots. Serve immediately.

24 June 1811
The Magiſtrates acting for this Hundred
have given peremptory Order to the
Conſtables and other Peace Officers to
apprehend all Common Beggars Ballad
Singers and other Vagrants ſo that the
may be dealt with according to Law.
60

Goat Milk Mousse and Sorrel Sorbet

Serves 4

Ingredients

Sorrel sorbet

45 g inverted sugar
45 g water
5 g glycerine
juice of half an orange
juice of half a lemon
1 bunch of sorrel

- Mix all the ingredients together in a blender until smooth.
- Freeze, and then re-blend in an ice cream machine. Alternatively, place into a plastic tub in the freezer and as it starts to freeze, fork the frozen ice to make granules (this would form a granita rather than a sorbet).

Goat milk mousse

25 g goat curd
60 g double cream
12 g sugar
140 g good quality goat milk

- Warm the ingredients together on low heat.
- Add the soaked gelatine leaves (soaked in cold water until soft). Blend with a small stick blender until it thickens.
- Pour into a cream-whipper and chill upside down at 4°C for 4 hours until ready.
- To serve, add a gas cartridge to the whipper, pipe out the whipped goat milk mousse into frozen glasses and then add the sorrel sorbet in the middle with a mini sorrel leaf to garnish.

Jerusalem Artichoke Soup

Serves 4

Ingredients

Soup

1 kg Jerusalem artichokes, washed
1 clove of garlic, chopped
3 sticks of celery, medium-chopped
1 onion, peeled and medium-chopped
1 medium floury potato
2 litres chicken or vegetable stock, warmed
300 ml warmed double cream
50 g salted butter
salt and freshly ground pepper

To garnish

Artichoke crisps
25 g toasted hazelnuts

- Scrub the artichokes and chop into small pieces.
- Sweat in a hot pan with butter and oil with the chopped onion, garlic and celery.
- Add stock and chopped potato. Cook until soft.
- Liquidise in a blender with the warmed cream. Season to taste.
- Pass through a sieve.
- Garnish with toasted hazelnuts and artichoke crisps.

Chef's tip — when selecting artichokes, choose those that are less gnarled as they will contain fewer pockets for dirt and grit to collect. To garnish, use some very finely sliced and deep-fried artichoke crisps or a few pan-fried scallops.

Ravioli of Guinea Fowl with Wild Mushrooms and Sage Beurre Noisette

Serves 4

Ingredients

Pasta

275 g pasta flour
6 egg yolks
4 whole eggs
1 tbsp olive oil
1 tbsp Maldon salt
a pinch of saffron strands infused in a little hot water

- Mix all the ingredients together in a bowl.
- Turn out onto a floured surface.
- Knead by hand for 10 minutes.
- Rest the dough for 30 minutes in the refrigerator.
- Divide the pasta dough into four. Run the pasta through the machine in sections until the desired thickness is achieved.

Ravioli filling

2 guinea fowl breasts, skinned and boned
1 shallot
100 ml double cream to blend
150 g wild mushrooms
1 bunch sage, chopped
75 g salted butter
salt and freshly ground pepper

- Purée the guinea fowl breast with the cream in a food processor.
- Sauté finely diced shallots, garlic and wild mushrooms.
- Leave to cool.
- Pass the guinea fowl mix through a fine sieve to remove any sinew.
- Fold in the mushrooms and mix with the guinea fowl and season.

Ravioli

- Roll out the sheets of pasta.
- Place a spoonful of the guinea fowl mixture down the middle of the sheet.
- Brush around each spoonful with a beaten egg.
- Roll out another sheet of the pasta and place on top.
- Gently form individual portions by cupping portions with both hands.
- Use 3 ascending size round cutters. Place the smallest and the next size inside each other and press upside down on to the pasta portions. This will form a neat little edge to the ravioli.
- With the largest cutter put the right way up, cut out the rounds to finish
- Place onto a floured tray
- Rest the ravioli in a refrigerator for 30 minutes.

To serve

Cook the ravioli in boiling salted water with a splash of olive oil for around 4 minutes. Remove with a slotted spoon and plate up into a large white bowl. Meanwhile, in a hot pan, add the diced salted butter. Wait until it foams and colours nut brown to form beurre noisette (brown butter), then add the chopped sage. Spoon a little of the beurre noisette over the ravioli to finish. Serve.

Fillet of John Dory, Crab and Scallop Boudin, Tomato Terrine and Avocado Cream

Serves 4

Ingredients

4 fillets of John Dory

Crab and scallop boudin

1 ½ large scallops
66 g white picked crab
2 tbsp double cream
Maldon salt
Cayenne pepper
baby courgettes

- Chill the food processor bowl until ice cold.
- Place the scallops and salt inside and purée until smooth.
- Pass through a drum sieve and place back into the cold, clean food processor.
- Add double cream and blend until a smooth consistency is reached.
- Season with salt, lemon juice and cayenne pepper.
- Add in the crab meat.
- Roll into boudins, wrap in kitchen film and poach at 55 °C for 10 minutes in a pan of hot water.
- Once poached, remove and leave to cool, then cut out from film.
- Slice the baby courgettes finely, wrap each boudin and roll in kitchen film to maintain the shape. Reheat on service.

Tomato terrine

1 kg good quality red tomatoes
15 g white balsamic vinegar
½ gelatine leaf
4 g basil
1 bunch tarragon
¼ head of fennel
1 tsp diced shallot
salt and sugar to taste

- Blanch the tomatoes petals down but retain the seeds and trim.
- Season the petals with salt and sugar and leave to dry for 12 hours on cooling racks.
- Take the seeds and add 3 g of basil, all of the tarragon, the shredded fennel and sliced shallots, then season and marinate for 12 hours.
- After 12 hours, line the required mould with double cling film and begin to build the terrine.
- Taste the tomatoes and check how much seasoning is required.
- Layer the tomatoes, seasoning each layer and brushing it with white balsamic.
- Place on top of terrine, weigh down and leave to press for at least 10 hours.
- Take the marinated tomato seeds and pulse in the food processor and then pass through muslin.
- Take the gelatine leaves and soak.
- Take 60 g of tomato essence, season with 10 g of white balsamic, then season to taste with sugar and salt.
- Weigh 10 g of liquid and 1 g of basil, bring to a boil and melt gelatine.
- Pass through a fine sieve and mix with the rest of the weighed-out tomato essence. Set a thin layer on top of the terrine and refrigerate to set
- When the terrine has set, it can be cut into portions.

Avocado cream

½ avocado
10 g double cream
a pinch of salt
1 tsp lime juice
3 drops Tabasco

- Peel and stone the avocado.
- Place the avocado and a pinch of salt in a blender and blend until smooth.
- Add the cream, salt, lime juice and Tabasco.
- Pass through a fine sieve, check the seasoning and place in piping bags ready to serve.

Ratatouille

½ yellow courgette
½ green courgette
½ red pepper
olive oil
Maldon salt

- Brunoise all vegetables then sweat in olive oil with Maldon salt.
- Add the courgettes and season again, then quickly remove from the pan and leave to cool on a tray.

White wine shallots

100 g brunoised shallots
150 g white wine
20g wine vinegar
salt

- Sweat the shallots with a little salt, making sure they have no colour left.
- Add the vinegar and reduce until dry, then add the white wine and reduce again until dry.

Lemon dressing

32 g lemon juice
4 g white wine vinegar
zest of ½ a lemon
48 g olive oil
1 g sugar
1 g salt

- Place all the ingredients except the oil into a bowl. Whisk in the oil to emulsify.

To serve

Place a slice of the tomato terrine onto a chilled plate. Dot some avocado cream on top of the terrine and to the side. Mix your vegetable dice with the white wine shallots and a bit of the lemon dressing. Re-heat the boudin in a pan of simmering water for 30 seconds. Cut from kitchen film and pop onto your plate. Pan-fry the John Dory fillets in a pan with some oil until just cooked. Place the fillets on the plate and sprinkle the dressed vegetables around and between the other ingredients

Mango and Coconut Mousse, Lime Sherbet and Lime Gel

Serves 6

Ingredients

Mango mousse

180 g mango purée
25 g Crème de Banane liqueur
Juice from half a lime
2 bronze gelatine leaves

- Firstly soak the gelatine in water, then warm 10 g of mango purée. Melt the gelatine and pass through a fine sieve onto the rest of the mango purée and mix.
- Season with lime and Crème de Banane liqueur.
- Pour into a cream whipper, charge with gas, shake and leave to set.

Coconut mousse

180 g coconut purée
25 g Malibu
Juice from half a lime
1.5 bronze gelatine leaves

- Soak the gelatine in water, warm 10 g coconut purée and melt the gelatine.
- Pass through a sieve onto the rest of the coconut purée.
- Season with Malibu and lime juice.
- Pour into a cream whipper, charge with gas, shake and then leave to set.

Lime sherbet

150 g thick Greek yogurt
50 g whole milk
2 lime leaves
20 g caster sugar
3 g glycerine
10 g acid yogurt powder
20 g inverted sugar
Juice of 1 lime
zest of half a lime

- Place milk and lime leaves in a vacuum bag and infuse for 12 hours at 80°C.
- Mix all ingredients together and blend to emulsify.
- Place in an ice cream machine and churn till smooth.

Toasted coconut tubes

10 slices of thin white bread
½ coconut, grated
25 g white chocolate pistols
50 g clarified butter
Icing sugar shaker
stainless steel tubes, 2.5 cm in diameter and 50 cm in length

- Trim the crusts off the bread and roll the bread through a pasta machine on its widest setting.
- Brush with clarified butter and lightly dust with icing sugar.
- Roll the thin bread sheets around stainless steel tubes lined with greaseproof paper and place on tray with the fold at the bottom.
- Separate the tubes with rings to stop movement and bake at 160°C until golden brown.
- Once baked, leave to cool and remove the bread cylinders from tubes.
- Grate the fresh coconut and toast in the oven at 160°C until lightly golden. Turn the coconut every 5 minutes.
- Melt the white chocolate and brush it over the bread tubes. Roll the tubes in toasted coconut. The tubes should be generously coated and kept in sealed plastic containers ready for use.

Crystallised lime zest

2 limes, zested
caster sugar to brush

- Zest the limes.
- Add the caster sugar gently, rubbing it in with your fingers until it reaches the correct consistency.
- The lime zest should then be left to air dry on parchment paper.

Lime gel

35 g fresh lime juice
20 g caster sugar
20 g water
6 g Vege-Gel
1 lime leaf

- Place the sugar, water and lime leaf in a pan and bring to a boil, then leave to infuse.
- Once cool, add the Vege-Gel and 13 g of lime juice.
- Place on stove and bring to a simmer, whisking as it increases in temperature.
- Pour the liquid quickly into a container and leave to set.
- When set, place the mixture in a blender and blend till smooth, adding the remaining lime juice.

To garnish

1 fresh Alphonso mango, peeled and diced into small pieces
Fresh coriander cress

To serve

Pipe both flavours of mousse into the bread tubes. Arrange a few on each plate. Dot some lime gel around each plate. Place a scoop of sherbet on each plate. Garnish with a dice of fresh mango and coriander cress.

Honey, Saffron and Pollen Bread

21 x 50 g rolls

Ingredients

600 g strong white bread flour, sieved
1 pinch of table salt
1½ tbsp perfumed honey
2 tbsp pollen grains
1 pinch saffron strands infused in a little hot water
25 g fresh yeast
450 ml lukewarm water
1 tbsp crème fraîche

- Preheat oven till 250°C.
- Mix the yeast, a little of the honey and water together, leave in a warm place until a foam forms on top (approximately 20–25 minutes).
- Strain off the saffron liquor.
- Place the sieved strong flour into a mixing bowl with a pinch of salt. Add honey, saffron, liquor, pollen grains and crème fraîche.
- Slowly add the yeast mixture to the flour until the dough is sticky and pliable. Place in a mixing machine with the dough hook (this process can be done by hand; it just takes a little longer).
- Form your dough into a ball on a floured surface, return to the floured mixing bowl and cover with a damp tea towel. Leave in a warm place until the mixture has doubled in size.
- Take the mixture out of the bowl and knead and fold for approximately eight minutes until the dough forms a more manageable elastic texture.
- Divide the dough into 50 g pieces and, using a cupped hand, gently roll in a circular motion to form a bread roll.
- Place into greased and floured dariole moulds.
- Return to a warm spot until the dough has doubled once more.
- Bake immediately in a preheated oven for approximately 12 minutes.
- Leave to cool in the tins for two minutes and gently lift out of the moulds onto a metal cooling wire.

Chef's tip — using a tall metal dariole mould gives the bread an interesting shape similar to that of a flower pot. The crème fraîche gives the bread an extra gloss and lightness.

Pan-fried Isle of Skye Scallop, Seaweed Jelly, Pickled Radish and Mouli and Wasabi Foam

Serves 6

Ingredients

6 large fresh scallops
1 bag dried, mixed, edible seaweed
6 breakfast radishes, washed and sliced thinly on their long side

Seaweed jelly

10 g dried sweet kombu
250 g water
15 g lemongrass
4 g ginger
1.5 g yuzu chilli paste
4 g galangal
Juice of half a lime
20 g mirin
½ tsp sesame oil
3 g tamari soya sauce
(preferably Clear Springs Cedar, aged)
1 tsp yuzu juice
20 g Mizkan rice vinegar
175 g of liquid to 1 leaf of gelatine

- Soak the kombu with water, lemongrass, ginger, yuzu paste and galangal for half an hour. Bring to 83 °C and let it cool. Cover and leave to infuse for 24 hours.
- Pass through a fine cloth and add the lime juice, mirin, sesame oil, tamari soya sauce, yuzu juice, rice vinegar and gelatine. Leave refrigerated to set.

Wasabi foam

500 g fish stock
250 g white wine
250 g milk
50 g double cream
5 g lecithin
8 g wasabi paste
50 g lime juice
6 g salt

(Blend all ingredients with a stem blender. Use just the foam created after each blending. For best results, bring your liquid to a near simmer before blending.)

Pickled mouli

⅓ mouli
50 g mirin
25 g Mizkan rice vinegar
25 g water
25 g lime juice
1 lime leaf
Pinch of salt and sugar

- Peel the mouli and thinly slice on a mandolin. Use a cutter to cut out perfect circles from your slices. Allow seven per portion.
- Bring the mirin, Mizkan rice vinegar, water, lime juice, lime leaf, salt and sugar to simmer for 2 minutes and then leave to cool.
- Add the mouli disks.

To serve

Lightly pan-fry the scallops in a little olive oil to caramelise the outside surfaces. Do this for 2–3 minutes depending on their size. Arrange the mouli discs on the centre of the plate. Season the discs with a little sea salt, then place a little soaked seaweed on each plate. Place two teaspoons of the jelly on the plates. Finish with the cooked scallop, sliced radish and wasabi foam. Serve immediately.

Pan-fried Skate Wing, Purple Cauliflower Purée, Pickled Cauliflower and Romanesco, Caper and Citrus Butter Sauce

Serves 4

Ingredients

4 medium-sized skate wings
1 large lemon
1 tbsp capers
1 large purple cauliflower
1 small white cauliflower
1 small Romanesco
approx. 50 g butter and olive oil for frying
200 ml milk
100 ml double cream
1 large bag washed baby spinach
100 ml cider vinegar
1 pinch caster sugar

- Cut the purple cauliflower into florets, place in a pan with the milk and cream and cook until soft. Liquidise until smooth and season to taste.
- Place the white cauliflower florets and Romanesco florets in boiling salted water. Remove while still a little crunchy.
- Pop them into the cider vinegar and caster sugar mix.
- Wilt the spinach in a hot pan with a little butter and season.
- Pan-fry the skate wings till golden brown on both sides. Finish in a hot oven if necessary.
- Place the capers, chopped lemon segments and juice with the butter from the skate pan.

To serve

Spread a little purple purée onto each plate. Scatter a few pickled florets on each plate, followed by a small mound of the spinach. Finish with a skate wing, per portion, topped with a little golden citrus and caper butter.

Rice Pudding with Toasted Coconut, Mango, Lime Syrup and Gorse Flowers

Serves 6

Ingredients

Rice pudding

300 ml double cream
225 g short grain rice
1.2 litre cold milk
100 g caster sugar
50 g butter
8 egg yolks
fresh coconut

- Place the rice in cold water in a covered bowl. Bring to a boil, then drain and refresh.
- Boil 1 litre of the milk, half the sugar and all of the butter in a large pan with the rice.
- Bring to a simmer and cook for 8–10 minutes until tender.
- Beat the egg yolks and the other half of sugar together in a bowl.
- Boil cream with remaining milk and pour onto the yolks, stirring all the time with the rice.
- Cook gently on low heat until it thickens.

Lime syrup

100 g caster sugar
100 ml water
2 limes, juiced
gorse flowers, washed gently (optional)
1 ripe mango

- Place sugar, water and lime juice in a small pan. Place on heat and reduce until thick and syrupy.
- Peel the mango and cut into small chucks. Place in a small pan with a little sugar and a dash of water and poach gently for five minutes.
- Crack open the fresh coconut and cut into thin strips using a vegetable peeler. Toast under a hot grill.
- Grate and toast a small amount of coconut flesh to garnish.

To serve

Serve the rice pudding in a fancy bowl with the lime syrup, fresh mango and toasted coconut. Scatter a few gorse flowers on it if available.

Chefs tip - this rice pudding can be changed to suit your own taste by finishing with a spoon of homemade fruit jam instead of the mango, coconut and lime syrup. For the summer months, crystallised rose petals and rosewater would be a delightful alternative.

Quince Jelly

Approx. 1 kg

Ingredients

1 kg quince, rinsed and roughly chopped (no need to peel or core)
1 vanilla pod, split
1 strip (½ inch by 2 inches) of lemon peel (only the yellow peel, no white pith)
1 ½ tbsp lemon juice
about 500 –750 g granulated sugar (exact amount will be determined during cooking)

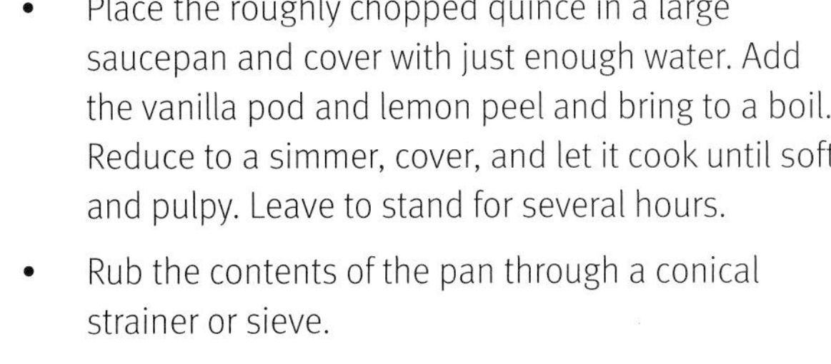

- Place the roughly chopped quince in a large saucepan and cover with just enough water. Add the vanilla pod and lemon peel and bring to a boil. Reduce to a simmer, cover, and let it cook until soft and pulpy. Leave to stand for several hours.
- Rub the contents of the pan through a conical strainer or sieve.
- Weigh the quince pulp and return to a clean pan, adding an equal weight of granulated sugar.
- Bring gently to a boil, stirring with a wooden spoon until the sugar has completely dissolved. Add the lemon juice.
- Simmer for an hour and to an hour and a half until thick, glossy and a rich amber-pink colour. The mixture is ready when it is so thick that you are able to run a spoon through it and see the base of the pan.
- Line an 8x8 baking pan with parchment paper. Grease the parchment paper with a thin coating of butter. Pour the cooked quince into the parchment paper-lined baking pan.
- To serve, cut into squares or wedges and present with Manchego cheese (matured cheese preferred) or to accompany your cheese board with handmade crackers, walnut and sultana bread.
- Store by wrapping in foil or plastic wrap and keeping in the refrigerator. Eat within 12 months.

Marcello Tully

The head chef at Kinloch Lodge has been collecting accolades from the day he took his first professional steps in a kitchen at the age of 14. After college, Marcello Tully caught the attention of French restaurateur Albert Roux, who took him under his wing at UK restaurant Home Rouxl, where he was named the head chef at age 23. After working at Le Gavroche, Rouxl Britannia and La Boucherie Lamartine, the Brazilian-born chef moved into the catering industry. He has stayed true to his Scottish roots and uses local produce to great effect. Kinloch Lodge, which is on the Isle of Skye, won a Michelin Star in 2010 and three AA rosettes in 2009. It is one of only seven in Scotland to be awarded the Michelin Guide's Red Grape for their wine list. Tully is a member of the Master Chefs of Great Britain.

Menu 1

Goat Cheese with Fig and Onion Tart and Sesame Seed Dressing

Marinated Chicken in Honey and Yogurt with Couscous

Panna Cotta

Menu 2

Apple and Blue Cheese Salad with Spicy Gazpacho Water

Salmon with Tomato and Orange Dressing

Bread and Butter Pudding

Menu 3

Home-cured Salmon with Beetroot and Crème Fraîche

Chicken Supreme with Lightly Spiced Honey and Vegetable Mousse

Apple and Calvados Cheesecake

Menu 4

Tiger Prawns with Spicy Herb Butter

Brazilian Feijoada

Lemon Tart

Menu 5

Aubergine Gateâu

Taste of the Isles

Passion Fruit Parfait

Goat Cheese with Fig and Onion Tart and Sesame Seed Dressing

Serves 4

Allow 1 round of goat cheese 1cm in depth for the topping of each tart.

Ingredients

Relish

(4 x 35 g portions)

20 g sunflower oil
120 g sliced onions
130 g chopped fresh figs
25 g balsamic vinegar
15 g caster sugar
2 drops Tabasco

- Heat oil and fry onions until golden brown.
- Add chopped figs, balsamic vinegar and sugar.
- Cook until most of the liquid has evaporated.
- Add Tabasco.

Pastry

(8–10 pastry rounds)

100 g plain flour
40 g grated Parmesan
⅓ tsp pink peppercorns
½ tsp salt
16 g walnuts
55 g butter

- In a blender, mix the Parmesan, peppercorns, salt and walnuts; then add flour.
- Combine with softened butter and chill for 1 hour before use.
- On a lightly floured work surface, roll the pastry out and use a 2-inch round pastry cutter to make the rounds. Use a palette knife to gently lift the pastry onto a baking tray which does not require greasing.
- Bake at 150°C for 8 minutes.
- Allow to cool and then use a palette knife to remove from the tray.

Sesame seed dressing

(makes 400 ml)

2 tbsp Dijon mustard
2 tbsp caster sugar
2 egg yolks
200 g sunflower oil
250 g hazelnut oil
2 tbsp white wine vinegar
150 g sesame seeds
salt and pepper to taste

- In a large bowl, whisk the mustard and sugar together with the egg yolks and vinegar.
- Gradually whisk in a steady trickle of oil, making sure the oil is well emulsified.
- Heat a small, dry frying pan and add the sesame seeds. Keep moving the seeds for 2–3 minutes with a wooden spoon until they become lightly golden.
- Allow to cool and then mix into the dressing.

To serve

You will need four 2-inch pastry cutters to build the tartlets. Using the same pastry cutter as before, cut rounds from the sliced goat cheese. Place a baked pastry round at the base of each cutter, gently warm the relish and place a dessert spoon on the pastry base. Using the spoon, level the relish off. Place another pastry round on top and lay the goat cheese round on top. Remove the cutter and, using a blow torch, gently brown the cheese. Transfer the tart to a serving plate, arrange a small sprig of salad leaves and drizzle the dressing around the plate.

Marinated Chicken in Honey and Yogurt with Couscous

Serves 4

Ingredients

Couscous

240 g couscous
420 g water
12 g rapeseed oil
120 g diced red onion
5 g garlic, finely chopped
1 g ground cumin
6 g salt
96 g cooked whole chickpeas
50 g sultanas
40 g dried apricots, roughly chopped
5 g coriander, roughly chopped
120 g red pepper, cut into small dice
90 g cooked green beans

- Heat the oil in a heavy-based pan and sweat off the onions for 5 minutes.
- Add the ground coriander, ground cumin, salt, water, chickpeas, sultanas and apricots and bring to a boil.
- Add the red peppers and green beans.
- Add the couscous, cover with a lid, turn off the heat.
- Leave for 10 minutes and then chill.

Marinated chicken

385 g chicken breasts (cut into 1-inch cubes)
3 g salt
40 g water
3 g cornflour
1 g fresh thyme, roughly chopped
7 g fresh coriander, roughly chopped
1 g crushed black pepper
25 g sunflower oil
1 g ground turmeric
1 g ground coriander
1 g ground cumin
1 g fresh garlic, finely chopped
3 g clear honey
13 g natural yogurt

- Cut the chicken fillets into 1-inch cubes and place in a bowl.
- Add all the remaining ingredients and mix gently.
- Allow to marinate overnight in the fridge.
- Place into a baking dish and cook for 15 minutes at 175° C.
- Allow to cool.

To serve

Place the cubed chicken on top of the couscous.

Panna Cotta

Serves 8 (individual portions of 65 g)

Ingredients

2 gelatine leaves
2 tbsp milk
250 ml double cream
250 ml crème fraîche
100 g caster sugar
1 vanilla pod

- Dilute the gelatine leaves in the milk for 10 minutes.
- In a heavy-based pan, add the double cream, crème fraîche, milk from the gelatine leaves, vanilla pod and sugar and stir.
- Heat to just under boiling point and remove from heat. Stir in the gelatine leaves.
- Divide into portions as desired—pour into small ramekins or use all the mix in one mould.
- Set in the fridge for 6 hours before decanting and serving.

Apple and Blue Cheese Salad with Spicy Gazpacho Water

Serves 4

Ingredients

½ apple (Gala or Braeburn)
20 g blue cheese
a handful of mixed salad leaves
6 crushed pistachios

- Crush the pistachios roughly in a mortar and pestle.
- Crumble the blue cheese into a bowl.
- Peel and core the apple and then cut into small dices.
- Mix all the ingredients together.
- Serve with sesame seed dressing.

Iced Gazpacho Water

(makes 16 Shots)
1 cucumber, roughly chopped
2 red peppers, roughly chopped
3 tomatoes, roughly chopped
2 punnets cherry tomatoes, whole
2 cloves fresh garlic, roughly chopped
50 ml vodka
50 ml water
A pinch of saffron
2 drops Tabasco
4 g caster sugar
50 ml white wine vinegar
3 g salt
a dash of Worcestershire sauce
1 white muslin cloth
Shot glasses

- Put all the vegetables in a food processor or liquidiser and blitz to a pulp.
- Add all the remaining ingredients and blitz again.
- Place the pulp into a muslin cloth and gather up the corners, then tie with a piece of string.
- Transfer the muslin to the fridge, suspending it with a piece of string from the shelf, this will allow the liquid inside the muslin to gently seep through. Put a dish directly underneath to collect the liquid.
- Leave overnight.
- Fill three-fourths of the shot glass with water and freeze.
- Just before serving, transfer the Gazpacho liquid into a jug, give it a very gentle stir and pour on top of the ice in the shot glass.

Salmon with Tomato and Orange Dressing

Serves 5

Ingredients

5 x 125 g salmon fillets (with the skin on)
100 g olive oil
5 g salt
2 g ground coriander
5 g orange/lemon rind
320 g beef tomato
15 g basil, finely chopped
200 g baby spinach leaves

Dressing

- Skin the beef tomatoes by submerging them very quickly in a pan of boiling water. Allow them to cool a little before handling and peel off the skin. Cut into quarters and remove the seeds. Cut into medium-sized dice pieces.
- Slice the lemon very thinly and cut the orange rind into thin strips. Blanch these in boiling water for 1–2 minutes, then remove and let it drain.
- Mix the olive oil, salt, ground coriander, orange and lemon rind and beef tomatoes.
- Just before serving the dressing, mix in the fresh, chopped basil.

Bed of spinach

- Wash the spinach thoroughly and let it drain for a few minutes.
- In a large thick-based pan, add a little sunflower oil and heat.
- When the pan is very hot, add the spinach very quickly and stir immediately. Remove from the pan and let it drain once again, ideally in a sieve.

Fish

- Season the salmon with salt and pepper then lightly fry, skin side down first, so that the skin becomes crispy. Do this for around 3–4 minutes either side.

To serve

Place the spinach on the base of the plate, then sit the salmon fillet on top. Spoon over the dressing and serve.

Bread and Butter Pudding

Serves 5–6

INGREDIENTS

850 g de-crusted white bread
125 g milk
165 g double cream
½ a vanilla pod
½ g salt
80 g butter
2 eggs
50 g sugar
3/4 shot of rum
30 g raisins

- Soak the raisins in rum overnight.
- Split the vanilla pod in half and place in a heavy-based saucepan with milk, cream, salt and butter and bring to a boil. Then remove from heat.
- Whisk the eggs and sugar in a large bowl until thick and fluffy.
- Whisk the milk mix into the eggs and sugar.
- Pour onto the bread, add the rum-soaked raisins and mix.
- Grease an oven-proof dish or loaf tin.
- Pour the mix into the dish/tin.
- Cook in a bain-marie in a preheated oven at 160°C for 45 minutes.

Home-cured Organic Salmon with Beetroot and Crème Fraîche

Serves 8

Ingredients

1 kg organic salmon, boned and skinned
400 g sugar and 300 g salt mixed together to cure the salmon
200 g raw beetroot
salt and pepper for seasoning
a splash of Tabasco
2 tbsp crème fraîche

To cure the salmon

Rub the salmon side with the salt and sugar mix and wrap in cling film. Leave overnight to cure. Then wash the salmon thoroughly and let it drain. Place in the fridge for a short while before serving.

- Wrap the raw beetroot individually in foil and cook in the oven for 1 ½ hours. Remove and cool to a temperature where it can be handled, preferably with gloves.
- Peel the beetroot and cut into small cubes, then season with salt, pepper and Tabasco. Mix in the crème fraîche.
- If required, you can shred some of the beetroot very finely and deep fry just before serving.

Chicken Supreme with Lightly Spiced Honey and Vegetable Mousse

Serves 8–10

Ingredients

Outer chicken mousse

(makes 7–8 portions)

140 g aubergine/courgette, peeled and finely diced
5 g garlic
145 g chicken breast without skin
1 egg
5 g salt
220 g double cream

- Fry the aubergine or courgette with garlic in oil for approximately 5 minutes till cooked and tender, but do not allow to brown.
- Put the aubergine or courgette and garlic in a food processor and blend, then add the chicken breast and blend to a smooth paste.
- Add the egg and salt and blend further.
- Add the double cream and blend until a smooth mousse is obtained, taking care not to over-blend or the mousse will split.

Middle mousse

(makes 10–12 portions)

70 g julienne of carrot
120 g julienne of celery
100 g julienne of courgette
20 g butter
4 g salt
20 g honey
chilli powder to taste
130 g chicken breast
1 egg white
150 g whipped cream

- Melt the butter in a pan and add the julienne of carrots and celery, sweat quickly. Then add the julienne of courgettes, chilli powder, salt and honey and mix well. Remove to cool (the vegetables should be cooked but still crunchy).
- Place the de-nerved chicken breast into a food processor and blitz to a pulp, then add the egg white and salt and blend again. Lastly, add the cream. Make sure the consistency is smooth. When cool, mix the vegetables with the mousse.

For the garnish: 3–4 pieces of steamed diced butternut (3 g per portion)

Spinach pancakes

(makes 6 portions)

130 g plain flour
3 eggs
170 ml milk
80 g cooked spinach, drained and squeezed
salt and pepper to taste
sunflower oil

- Fry the clean spinach in a little oil (approximately 20 ml) in a very hot, heavy-based pan.
- Drain the spinach thoroughly and squeeze the remaining juice from the leaves.
- Whisk the eggs and flour together and add the milk.
- Chop the spinach finely and add to the mix.
- Add salt and pepper to season.
- Heat a little oil in a small frying pan (approximately 1 tsp) add a ladle of pancake mixture.
- Even the mixture out in the pan so that it covers the whole surface. Cook for 1–2 minutes.
- Turn over and cook for a further minute.
- Repeat this procedure until all the mix is finished.
- Allow the pancakes to cool.

Sweetcorn espuma

(makes 1 litre; 50 g sauce to be used per portion)

¼ onion (finely chopped)
1 ½ g sunflower oil
¼ tbsp ground turmeric
1 kg tin sweet corn
800 ml water
500 ml double cream
sugar to taste
salt to taste
Tabasco to taste

- Heat the oil in a heavy-based pan and add the chopped onions and turmeric. Sweat for 2–3 minutes without browning the onions.
- Add the entire content of the sweetcorn tin into the pan and add the measured water.
- Bring to a boil and let it simmer for five minutes.
- Blitz the soup in a food processor at medium speed but do not go any higher.
- Now the soup is ready to be passed through a sieve. Use the back of a ladle to gently squeeze the mix through.
- Place the sieved soup in a clean pan and add the double cream. Bring to a boil and add the seasoning (sugar, salt and Tabasco).
- Pour the soup into a food processor once more and blitz at high speed until it has a silky smooth consistency.

Popcorn snow

500 g popcorn kernels
salt to taste
sunflower oil for frying

- Add the oil to a large pan and heat.
- Add the popcorn kernels and shake, then place lid on top. Shake the pan occasionally.
- When the kernels have stopped popping, remove from heat and place into a bowl to cool. Add the salt and mix well.
- Place the kernels into a food processor and blitz at high speed until a powder is achieved.

Wilted spinach

(makes 15 portions)

900 g baby leaf spinach
salt and pepper to taste
20 g sunflower oil

- Add the oil to a heavy-based pan and once the oil starts to smoke, add the spinach. Move it immediately.
- Allow the spinach to wilt and remove from the pan and into a colander to drain. Add the seasoning and gently mix.

To serve

Put a 125 g layer of outer mousse on the base of the terrine. Place a 150 g layer of vegetable mousse in the middle which has been piped onto the spinach pancake and rolled tightly to form a cylinder. Put 125 g outer mousse on top. Drizzle a thick spread of the sweetcorn espuma on a plate and on one end of the swatch, place the wilted spinach. Place the cylinder on top of the spinach. Fill a shot glass with the popcorn snow and place by the side of the plate.

Apple and Calvados Cheesecake

Serves 6–8

Ingredients

Sponge base

270 g caster sugar
10 whole eggs
270 g plain flour

- Whisk the eggs and caster sugar together until white and fluffy.
- Fold in the flour.
- Line a shallow baking tray with greaseproof paper.
- Pour the sponge mix into the tray and spread evenly.
- Cook in a preheated oven at 160°C for 8–10 minutes.
- Remove from the oven and let it cool.
- Using a circular pastry cutter, cut rounds from the sponge base and leave the sponge in the cutter to form the base of the cheesecake.

For the cheesecake

25 g butter
25 g caster sugar
150 g apples
50 ml apple juice
1 leaf of gelatine
125 g mascarpone cheese
100 g double cream
1 tsp vanilla essence
12 ml calvados

- Gently cook the sliced apples with butter, sugar and apple juice until all the liquid has reduced.
- Add the soaked gelatine to the apple mix when still warm.
- Add to a food processor and mix in all the other ingredients.
- Pour this cheesecake mix on top of the sponge base and place in the fridge for 4–6 hours to set.

Tiger Prawns with Spicy Herb Butter

Serves 4

INGREDIENTS

400 g large or medium raw prawns, peeled and de-veined
spice and herb butter
250 g salted butter softened
¼ fresh green chilli, deseeded and finely chopped
¼ fresh red chilli, deseeded and finely chopped
1 garlic clove, finely chopped
a small handful of fresh chopped coriander

- Mix the butter with the chillies, garlic and fresh coriander.
- In a frying pan, heat some of the herb butter and add the prawns. Fry for 1 minute, basting them in the butter as they cook.
- Remove and serve immediately with some crusty bread to help soak up the delicious juices.

Brazilian Feijoada

Serves 8–10

INGREDIENTS

750 g black beans
15 g salt
450 g diced pancetta
1 small pork tongue with the skin removed
450 g fresh pork sausages
450 g spareribs
600 g smoked sausages
2 pigs' feet
225 g lean bacon
1 tbsp oil
2 large chopped onions
3 crushed garlic cloves
4 g ground cumin

- Wash beans and soak in cold water overnight.
- Soak the tongue in water overnight.
- In the morning, drain the beans and cover with fresh cold water. Add the tongue, pigs' feet, bacon and spare ribs and cook for 2 ½ hours in a covered saucepan (add the pork sausage and garlic sausage 30 minutes towards the end of cooking). Keep adding water to ensure the beans are covered.
- About half an hour before serving, melt the oil in a large frying pan and gently sauté the onions and garlic, then add the cumin. Stir in 2 ladles of the beans and mash with a wooden spoon.
- Pour another 2 ladles of bean liquor into the mashed bean mix and simmer until the mixture thickens. Add this to the original pot of beans and meats and stir gently.

Traditionally, Feijoada is served with kale, but this can be substituted with cabbage or chicory. Serve with boiled rice. Like any good stew, Feijoada improves in flavour a day or two after it's made.

Lemon Tart

Serves 10

Ingredients

Shortbread

100 g butter
50 g icing sugar
1 egg
125 g plain flour
a pinch of salt
5 g vanilla essence

- Soften the butter.
- Add the icing sugar and salt.
- Add the egg yolks, flour and vanilla essence.
- Roll out the dough onto a flat surface and use a pastry cutter to shape into circles.
- Place on a greased baking tray.
- Bake for 6–8 minutes at 160°C and set aside to cool.

Lemon mix

Juice of 2 lemons
5 eggs
187 g caster sugar
150 ml double cream

- Whisk the egg yolks and caster sugar.
- Add lemon juice and double cream
- Cook the lemon mix in individual ramekins or pastry cutters lined with cling film to hold the mix in the cutter. Place in a bain-marie for 20 minutes.

To serve

Place the lemon mix on top of the shortbread biscuit and sprinkle icing sugar over it. With a blowtorch, caramelise the sugar to a golden brown.

Aubergine Gâteau

Serves 5

Ingredients

300 g sliced aubergine (257 g when fried)
80 g couscous
80 g water
3 g salt
110 g diced red pepper
100 g diced courgette
5 g fresh chopped parsley
5 g fresh chopped coriander
5 g finely chopped ginger
5 g finely chopped garlic
5 g chilli
10 g lemon juice

- Slice the aubergine and deep fry. Set aside.
- Put the couscous in a saucepan, add tepid water and salt and bring to a boil. Cover with a lid and turn off the heat.
- Place the peppers and courgettes in the oven (180°C) to roast for approximately 12 minutes.
- Gently fry the ginger, garlic and chilli for 1–2 minutes.
- Combine the couscous with the herbs, lemon juice, fried seasoning, courgette and red pepper.

To serve

Line the moulds with the sliced aubergine, ensuring each slice is slightly overlapping (approximately 45–50 g). Place 50 g of the couscous mix inside the mould and gently squeeze down so it takes the shape of the mould.

Taste of the Isles

Serves 5

Ingredients

Sauce

60 g onion
22 g leeks
50 g celery
40 g fennel
40 g carrots
55 g red peppers
2 g thyme
4 g garlic
8 g anchovy fillets, tinned and drained
250 ml fish stock
12 g tomato purée
125 g white-based fish (Whiting/plaice)
25 ml double cream
1 strand saffron
Tabasco to taste
Worcestershire sauce to taste
½ tsp white wine vinegar
½ tsp caster sugar

- Sweat off all the vegetables with the anchovies.
- Add tomato purée and let the mixture sweat for 2–3 minutes.
- Add fish stock and cook for 1 hour.
- Add the fish and cook for 10–15 minutes.
- Put this in a food processor and pass three-fourths of this mixture through a sieve.
- Add double cream, saffron, Tabasco, Worcestershire sauce, salt, sugar, garlic and white wine vinegar to taste.

Fish

(makes 5 portions)
5 x 150 g halibut
5 x ½ fillets sea bass
10 scallops
40 cooked mussels (2in the shell and 2 off the shell for each person)

To serve

Put the cooked halibut, sea bass, scallops and mussels together. Pour the sauce at the table around the components.

Passion Fruit Parfait

Serves 6–8

Ingredients

120 g caster sugar
3 whole eggs
8 3-inch silver rings
100 g double cream
75 g concentrated passion fruit purée

- Whisk the eggs with the caster sugar.
- Add the passion fruit purée and double cream and mix well.
- Line 6–8 3-inch silver rings with cling film on the base so the dessert cannot escape through the bottom. Pour 50 g into each ring.
- Preheat the oven to 160°C and cook the desserts in a bain-marie for 45 minutes or until set.
- Leave to cool.
- When cold, remove the cling film and, using a sharp knife, go round the ring and gently lift the ring off the dessert.

N.B. A bain-marie is a container such as a casserole dish or roasting tray which is half filled with simmering water. The food to be cooked is placed into the water within another container so that it doesn't touch the water directly. This method of cooking surrounds the food with very gentle heat and is used for cooking delicate dishes like custards, white sauces and melting of chocolate.

Passion fruit sauce for the topping

6 fresh passion fruit
150 g caster sugar

- To a heavy-based pan, add the pulp of the passion fruit (do this by cutting the fruit in half and removing all the seeds), then add the caster sugar.
- Heat and bring to a boil. Remove from heat when the sugar has dissolved and it has boiled for 3–5 minutes—until it has the consistency of syrup.
- Spoon on top of the passion fruit parfaits and serve.

Anand Kapoor

While putting Taste *together, I was asked by the publishers to incorporate some of my own recipes as well. My first reaction was to laugh as my cooking could not possibly be at par with chefs of such high calibre. But I eventually agreed to contribute my own food memories. I am not a chef; even classifying myself as an amateur cook would be a sacrilege. I am simply an individual who is passionate about food and loves cooking. Living away from home as I did, I hankered after home food. I decided I could either be miserable living out of takeaway containers or take matters into my own hands, literally. What follows are my personal recollections of food, from my grandfather's chicken korma to my interpretation of a delicious roast chicken and bread salad I had in San Francisco.*

Recipes

Chicken Korma

Comfort food handed down from my grandfather, this can either be made with chicken on the bone or boneless

Tea-infused Chickpeas

Much in demand every time it is cooked by my mother, it freezes very well and can be easily reheated for repeat tastings

Deconstructed Peanoffee Pie

A different take on the traditional banoffee pie, with liquorice cutting through the sweetness of the Dulce de Leche

Nana's Coffee Mousse Cake

From my godmother's recipe collection, a phenomenally moreish dish which is beautiful to look at and a winning combination of coffee and chocolate

Compote

A delicious dish from my aunt made without any butter or sugar; the Christmassy butterscotch taste goes perfectly with vanilla ice cream

Lasagne

My daughter's favourite—a lighter and healthier version of a usually calorie-heavy recipe

Roast Chicken with Bread Salad and Balsamic Bloody Mary

A complete meal that uses ingredients easily found in everyone's pantry, paired with a delightful entrée of a balsamic vinegar-infused Bloody Mary

Chicken Korma

Serves 4

INGREDIENTS

4 chicken breasts or one whole chicken cut into 8 pieces
4 large onions
250 g or half a large tub of natural yogurt
2 bay leaves
2 black cardamoms
2 green cardamoms
8 cloves
10 black peppercorns
1 medium stick of cinnamon
1 tsp salt
1 tsp red chilli powder
½ garlic bulb, minced
500 ml water
julienned fresh ginger
freshly chopped coriander

(If you have chosen to use boneless chicken, cut it into bite-size pieces)

- Place the chicken in a bowl and combine the yogurt, bay leaves, cardamoms, cloves, peppercorns, cinnamon, salt and chilli powder and mix well.
- Set aside to marinate for at least an hour. The longer it is left to marinate the better.
- Take the minced garlic and add to the 500 ml of room-temperature water. Again, the longer you leave this the flavour of the water improves.
- Finely chop the onions and put them in a generous amount of oil until they become dark brown and set aside. Be careful not to burn them.
- In the same pan, add the chicken and begin to cook it after 5–10 minutes depending on the size of the pieces. They will begin to go white and be partially cooked on the outside. Add the garlic water, enough to cover the pieces. Add salt to taste.
- Let the chicken simmer in the garlic water mix for 5 minutes and once it bubbles, add the fried onions. Stir them in well and let this simmer for about 20 minutes.
- Once the onions disappear and the sauce has thickened, it is ready to serve. You can keep the sauce as thick or loose as you like.
- Move to serving bowl and garnish generously with julienned ginger and chopped coriander. Serve with rice, naan or pita bread.

Tea-infused Chickpeas

Serves 8

Ingredients

500 g dried chickpeas
A pinch of soda bicarbonate
2 teabags
2 black cardamoms
1 medium piece cinnamon
2 bay leaves
1 tbsp garam masala
1 tbsp coriander powder
1 tbsp cumin powder
1–2 tsp red chili powder
4 large onions
5 garlic cloves, finely chopped
4 green chillies
1 cup corn oil
fresh ginger, julienned
freshly chopped coriander
1 red onion, sliced in circles
1 lemon

- Soak dried chickpeas overnight with enough water to cover them.
- In the morning, boil them in the water they had been soaking in. Add the soda bicarbonate, tea bags, black cardamoms, cinnamon stick and bay leaves. Boil till soft. The tea will impart its colour and a very subtle taste to the chickpeas.
- In a separate pan, fry onions till light brown. Add garam masala, coriander powder, red chilli powder and cumin powder. Briefly stir together to gently release their aroma.
- Add boiled chickpeas with their water after removing the tea bags. Fry all ingredients together.
- Once they have come to a gentle bubble, add garlic, ginger and green chillies.
- Cook on low heat after covering the pan for about 45 minutes or until the oil starts separating and rising to the top.
- While the chickpeas are cooking, slice the onions into circles and soak in cold water for at least 10 minutes and drain. Cut the lemon into wedges.
- Once the chickpeas are ready, put into a serving bowl and decorate with the circles of onions, lemon wedges, julienned chickpeas and chopped coriander. Serve with rice, naan or pita bread.

Deconstructed Peanoffee Pie

Serves 6–8

Ingredients

1 can evaporated milk or readymade Dulce de Leche (toffee)
1 tin peach halves
⅓ packet of digestive biscuits
83 g melted butter
100 ml whipping cream
10 pieces plain liquorice
fresh mint leaves
cocoa powder

- Remove label from can and pierce three holes in it (to release pressure from the heat and prevent it from exploding). Place the can in a saucepan filled with water three-quarters of the way up the side of the can.
- Bring water to a simmer and keep it there for at least 4 hours or until it reaches the desired consistency. When ready, carefully remove the can and let it cool slightly. Then place the Dulce de Leche in a bowl and whisk till smooth. Let it cool.
- While the Dulce de Leche is simmering, crush the digestive biscuits and combine with melted butter. Leave to set in the fridge.
- Whip up cream so it forms soft peaks and let this cool in the fridge.
- Take 5 tbsp syrup from the tin of peach halves and place in a saucepan with the liquorice.
- Simmer gently, allowing the liquorice to dissolve. Once done, set aside.
- Take the digestive biscuit mixture that will have set into a block and grate it.

To serve

Take a long plate and place half a peach at one end. Form a quenelle of the Dulce de Leche and place it next to the peach. Repeat the same process for the whipped cream. Take the digestive biscuit preparation and create a mound at the opposite end of the plate from the peach. Place a line of the liquorice syrup between each component on the plate. Add a sprig of mint to the top of the peach, sprinkle some cocoa powder on the quenelle of cream and serve. It may be easier to start with the peach and the digestive crumbs as it will allow you to evenly place the whipped cream and the Dulce de Leche.

Nana's Coffee Mousse Cake

Serves 8

INGREDIENTS

4 tbsp granulated sugar
4 eggs
125 g salted butter
400 g or two large bars of dark chocolate
300 ml whipping cream
1 cup strong black instant coffee
4 packets Marie biscuits
green food colouring (optional)
edible flowers

- Cream the butter together. Add the egg yolks and cream while retaining the egg whites.
- Melt the dark chocolate over a bain-marie and when it has cooled, stir in the egg yolk and sugar mixture.
- Whisk the egg whites and fold into the chocolate mixture. In another bowl, whip the cream and add half the whipped cream to the chocolate mixture.
- Line a dish with cling film. In a bowl, pour one mug hot, strong, instant coffee, take all the packs of Marie biscuits and dip each biscuit in coffee. Layer the dish with one layer of biscuits. Add the above cream mix. Continue to layer the dish till the coffee-dipped biscuits and cream are over. The top layer should be of the coffee-dipped biscuits.
- Fold cling film over it and chill till set. When set, remove cling film and turn out on a serving dish.
- Cover the cake with cream and decorate with the edible flowers.

Compote

Serves 4

Ingredients

10 dried apricots
10 figs
10 prunes
a handful of dried cranberries (optional)
a handful of dried cherries (optional)
125 g fresh strawberries
100 g of physalis fruit
1 vanilla pod
1 cinnamon stick
2 star anise
1 litre sweetened orange juice
a splash of brandy

- Add orange juice to a pan with the dried fruit, star anise, vanilla pod and cinnamon stick.
- Let it simmer on low heat till the fig and prunes begin to break down.
- While this is happening, wash and remove the stalks and leaves of the strawberries and physalis fruit. Then add the fresh fruit and brandy and let the fruit warm through.
- Remove from heat and serve in individual glasses with a scoop of vanilla ice cream.

Lasagne

Serves 6

Ingredients

Béchamel cheese sauce

5 tbsp butter
128 g all purpose flour
500 ml milk at room temperature
½ pint water
50 g cheddar cheese
salt and pepper
dried mixed Italian herbs or oregano and basil
chilli flakes

- Melt 5 tbsp butter over medium heat. When the butter has completely melted, add the flour and whisk until smooth, about two minutes. The consistency should be fairly loose.
- Gradually add the milk and water, whisking constantly to prevent any lumps from forming. The water helps lightens the sauce.
- Continue to simmer and whisk over medium heat until the sauce is thick, smooth and creamy; this takes about 10 minutes. The sauce should be thick enough to coat the back of the wooden spoon. Add the cheese, dried herbs, chilli flakes, salt and pepper to taste. Stir until well combined. Set aside and split into two equal portions.

Tomato sauce

250 g sliced mushrooms
5 tbsp extra virgin olive oil
1 large onion, chopped
6 garlic cloves, chopped
1 vegetable stock cube
1 bouquet garni
2 tins chopped tomatoes
1 kg chicken breast mince or extra lean beef mince or Quorn mince
salt and pepper
dried mixed Italian herbs or oregano and basil
chilli flakes
2 glasses red wine (optional)
700 ml water
a pinch of sugar

- In a large pan, heat olive oil over medium high heat. Fry the mince until cooked.
- Add sliced mushrooms, chopped onions and garlic and sauté until soft and translucent — about 5–10 minutes.
- Add salt and pepper, dried herbs, chilli flakes, the stock cube, the bouquet of garni, sugar, wine, chopped tomatoes and water.
- Simmer uncovered on low heat for an hour or until thick. Remove the bouquet of garni and check if it needs more seasoning.

To serve

100 g cheddar cheese (alternatively you can use 175 g and leave out the mozzarella and parmesan)
50 g mozzarella
25 g Parmesan
1 packet uncooked lasagne sheets
Olive oil
Fresh basil leaves

Take half the béchamel sauce and spread a layer of it onto the bottom of a baking dish. Arrange the pasta sheets side by side, covering the bottom of the dish. Evenly spread the tomato sauce mixture and, if using spinach, then a layer of the spinach. Drizzle some béchamel sauce and top with another layer of pasta. Repeat until you reach the top layer which should be pasta. Take the rest of the béchamel sauce and evenly pour it onto the layered lasagna. On top of this, arrange fresh basil leaves and sprinkle cheeses, dried herbs, chilli flakes and ground black pepper. Drizzle the top with olive oil. Cover with aluminium foil. Place the lasagne dish on the middle rack of the oven and bake until the top is bubbling — about 30 minutes. Remove the aluminium foil and continue to bake for about 30 minutes or until golden brown. The lasagne is ready.

Roast Chicken with Bread Salad and Balsamic Bloody Mary

Serves 2–3

Ingredients

one small chicken, 2-¾ to 3-½-pounds
4 tender sprigs fresh thyme, marjoram, rosemary, or sage (about ½ inch long)
about ¼ tsp freshly cracked black pepper
A little water
230 g slightly stale open-crumbed, chewy, peasant-style bread
6–8 tbsp mild-tasting olive oil
1 tsp red wine vinegar, or as needed
1 tbsp warm water
2 tbsp pine nuts
2–3 garlic cloves, slivered
4 slivered spring onions (scallions) including a little of the green part
2 tbsp lightly salted chicken stock or lightly salted water
a few handfuls of arugula, frisee or red mustard greens, carefully washed and dried
1½ tablespoons Champagne vinegar or white wine vinegar
1 tbsp dried currants

Seasoning the Chicken

(1 to 3 days before serving; for 3-¼- to 3-½-pound chickens, at least 2 days)

- Remove and discard the lump of fat inside the chicken. Rinse the chicken and pat dry inside and out.
- Approaching from the edge of the cavity, slide a finger under the skin of each breast, making two little pockets. Use the tip of your finger to loosen a pocket of skin on the outside of the thickest section of each thigh. Shove a herb sprig into all four pockets.
- Season the chicken liberally all over with salt and pepper (use ¾ teaspoon sea salt per pound of chicken). Season the thick sections more heavily than the skinny ankles and wings. Sprinkle just inside the cavity on the backbone. Twist and tuck the wing tips behind the shoulders. Cover loosely and refrigerate.

Preparing the Bread Salad

- Preheat the oven. Cut the bread into a couple of large chunks.
- Carve off the bottom crust and most of the top and side crusts (reserve the top and side crusts to use as croutons).
- Brush the bread all over with olive oil. Broil briefly to crisp and lightly colour the surface. Turn the chunks over and crisp the other side. Tear the chunks into a combination of 2- to 3-inch wads, bite-sized bits and fat crumbs. This should make about four cups.
- Combine about ¼ cup of the olive oil with the Champagne or white wine vinegar and salt and pepper to taste. Toss about ¼ cup of this vinaigrette with the bread in a wide salad bowl. Taste one of the more saturated pieces. If it is bland, add a little salt and pepper and toss again.
- Place the currants in a bowl and moisten with red wine vinegar and warm water. Set aside.

To Roast the Chicken and Assemble the Salad

- Preheat the oven to 475°C (depending on the efficiency of the oven and the size of the bird, you may need to adjust the heat to as high as 500°C or as low as 450°C to get the chicken to brown properly).
- Choose a shallow, flameproof roasting pan or dish barely larger than the chicken, or a 10-inch skillet with a metal handle. Preheat the pan over medium heat.
- Wipe the chicken dry and set it breast-side up in the pan. It should sizzle. Place in the centre of the oven and watch for it to start sizzling and browning within 20 minutes. If it doesn't, raise the temperature progressively until it does. The skin should blister, but if the chicken begins to char or the fat is smoking, reduce the temperature by 25°C.
- After about 30 minutes, turn the bird over. Roast for another 10–20 minutes, depending on the size, then flip back over to re-crisp the breast skin, another 5–10 minutes.

- While the chicken is roasting, place the pine nuts in a small baking dish and set in the hot oven for a minute or two. Add to the bowl of bread.
- Place a spoonful of olive oil in a small skillet, add the garlic and scallions and cook over medium-low heat, stirring constantly until softened. Don't let them colour. Scrape into the bread and fold to combine. Drain the plumped currants and fold in. Dribble the chicken stock or lightly salted water over the salad and fold again.
- Taste a few pieces of bread. If they are bland, add salt, pepper, and/or a few drops of vinegar, then toss well.
- Pile the bread salad in a 1-quart baking dish and tent with foil. Set the salad bowl aside. Place the salad in the oven after you flip the chicken one final time.

To serve

Remove the chicken from the oven and turn off the heat. Leave the bread salad to continue warming for another five minutes or so. Lift the chicken from the roasting pan and set on a plate. Carefully pour the clear fat from the roasting pan, leaving the lean drippings behind. Add about a tablespoon of water to the pan and swirl it.

Slash the stretched skin between the thighs and breasts of the chicken and tilt the bird and plate over the roasting pan to drain the juice into the drippings. Leave the chicken to rest in a warm spot while you finish the bread salad so the meat becomes more succulent. Set a platter in the oven to warm for a minute or two. Tilt the roasting pan and skim the last of the fat. Place over medium-low heat, add any juice that has collected under the chicken and bring to a simmer. Stir and scrape to soften any hard golden drippings. The juices should be extremely flavourful.

Tip the bread salad into the salad bowl. Drizzle and toss with a spoonful of the pan juices. Add the greens, a drizzle of vinaigrette, and fold well. Taste again. Cut the chicken into pieces, spread the bread salad on the warm platter and nestle the chicken in the salad.

Balsamic bloody mary

½ tbsp good quality balsamic vinegar
2 dashes Tabasco
1 shot vodka
2 grinds black pepper
1 tsp horseradish sauce
approx. 220 ml tomato juice
celery stick
salsa

- Put balsamic vinegar, Tabasco, black pepper, vodka, horseradish sauce, tomato juice and ice in a shaker.
- Shake well and pour into a tall glass.
- Add celery stalk and stir.
- Top glass with ice and garnish with salsa.